- **One birth every**
  United States . . .

- **Fifteen million births in China in 1958 . . . Six million in India . . . Three million six hundred thousand in Russia . . . Two million six hundred thousand in the United States . . .**

- **Each year the world's population increases and each year the rate of increase increases . . .**

WHAT CAN—OR SHOULD—BE DONE TO SLOW DOWN THE WORLD'S RAPIDLY INCREASING BIRTH RATE? In this vitally important book, three brilliant men consider this crucial question.

THOMAS MALTHUS, the world-famous nineteenth-century economist, presents his classic statement of the population problem.

JULIAN HUXLEY, the great biologist, surveys the status of the race between population and food production.

FREDERICK OSBORN, Chairman of the Executive Committee of the Population Council, discusses specific population problems faced by different areas of the world and outlines means of solving them.

Here is a pertinent and thought-provoking analysis of an urgent problem that concerns each and every one of us—and our descendants.

ON POPULATION

Three Essays

THOMAS MALTHUS

JULIAN HUXLEY

FREDERICK OSBORN

A MENTOR BOOK

Published by THE NEW AMERICAN LIBRARY

FIRST PRINTING, JUNE, 1960

MENTOR BOOKS are published by
The New American Library of World Literature, Inc.
501 Madison Avenue, New York 22, New York

PRINTED IN THE UNITED STATES OF AMERICA

CONTENTS

INTRODUCTION

The following three essays on population provide the general reader with a broad perspective on one of the most difficult problems of the modern world. One way of accomplishing this objective would have been to write a simplified account of the situation. We have preferred instead to let three outstanding students of population speak for themselves, retaining thereby the vigor and perception of the original works.

In a sense the selection is a curious one. It starts with a famous work of the Reverend Thomas R. Malthus, originally written, as if by another person, for the 1824 Supplement to the Encyclopaedia Britannica, and then published independently, revised and shortened, in 1830. From this classic discussion we jump to statements by two outstanding contemporary authorities: Sir Julian Huxley and Frederick Osborn. Well over a century of experience lies between the first and last two statements—a century that comprehends, on the one hand, almost the entire scientific and technological revolutions; and, on the other hand, a multiplication of the world's population by about two and one half times.

Our last two authors are members of British and American populations that have multiplied by five and thirty-five times, respectively, since Malthus's essay first appeared, and also achieved a state of general health, education and prosperity that Malthus would never have dreamed possible in this worldly "state of probation."

Huxley and Osborn, although citizens of prosperous nations, are primarily concerned with the population of the technologically underdeveloped nations which comprise much more than half of the world's present total. These populations have grown rather slowly since the beginning of the nineteenth century, and often present a picture of disease, illiteracy and poverty for the masses with which Malthus was wholly familiar.

The situation of these peoples is indeed what he deemed the chronic and almost necessary condition of the human race. Unchecked, Malthus said, populations tend to grow in a geometric progression and at a rate that would double the numbers about every twenty-five years. Food supplies at best, he thought, could increase in arithmetic progression. The superior power of population growth over the means of subsistence required that population growth would inevitably be checked, if not by preventive measures, then by the positive inroads of starvation, disease, war, etc. which he grouped under the heading of misery and vice.

His preventive checks to growth were continence and delayed marriage. By use of these prudential restraints, individuals and nations could reap the rewards of better living conditions. Human frailty was such, however, that only the threat of misery would induce such prudential restraint. Even with the threat of unrelieved poverty he was not very hopeful that the mass of the population would exercise sufficient restraint to avoid the positive checks, and the majority would inevitably live close to the margins of subsistence.

The source of the terrible living conditions was not, as the utopians claimed, the result of unjust social-economic institutions. It lay in the nature of the laws of a ". . . . benevolent Creator, which, while they furnish the difficulties and temptations which form the essence of such a stage [of worldly probation], are of such a nature as to reward those who overcome them, with happiness in this life as well as in the next."

This brief sketch is possibly sufficient to make it evident why Malthus and "Malthusianism" remain storm centers of intellectual and ideological strife. Now, there are very few strict Malthusians and clearly the present writer is not one of them. Yet the document is essential reading for anyone seeking either to understand the social-economic thought of the nineteenth century, or the resistance so frequently engendered in the underdeveloped countries when population problems are discussed in Malthusian terms.

His essay contains both fundamental truth and gross error. It is true that in a finite space nothing, including man, can increase without limit and indeed at current rates of growth the numbers would become fantastically large in a few generations. So far as the world as a whole is concerned, if population growth is to be reduced, the death rate must rise if the birth rate does not fall. Moreover, in any given period of time, man's living conditions are heavily influenced by the relation of basic resources to his numbers. Unquestionably the size and rate of growth of the population today are, as Malthus foresaw, major obstacles to the improvement of living conditions for more than half of the world's population.

On the other hand there are major errors—both in fundamental principles and in the practical proposals that grow out of his incomplete truths. He recognized that improved techniques of production and migration would mitigate the difficulties of population increase temporarily. But actually he neither foresaw, nor could have been expected to foresee, the tremendous burst of productivity that the following century brought forth. What to him were the possibilities of minor displacements from equilibrium became in the modern West more than a century of progressive release from the fundamental constraints with which he was preoccupied.

Malthus was no ivory-tower scholar. He was a political pamphleteer. He began the whole exercise as an attack on the poor laws. The poverty and suffering of the masses could not be aided by public relief. That would only stimulate population growth and make the situation worse. None of the plans of the utopian dreamers would work, because the difficulty arose, not from social injustice, but from natural law. Constantly throughout the nineteenth century the Malthusian argument was used to demonstrate the futility of every major reform in the social-economic field. Malthusiasm became an anathema to the reformers.

Malthus was also wrong in his estimate of the possibility of reducing fertility by preventive measures, although not by the ones he envisioned. He does not mention contraceptive practice explicitly, but if he knew about it he almost certainly would not have approved. He did not foresee the fact that Europe would reduce its birth rates drastically during the nineteenth and twentieth centuries through the spread of birth-control practices.

Finally, Malthus was wrong, so far as his social doctrine was concerned, in a basic assumption. At the heart of his doctrine is the view that only suffering and the threat of still worse suffering could be relied upon to induce restraint in the masses. Yet there is now clear evidence that abysmal poverty induces more of the same, and not prudence. The poorest must live just for the day to survive. Only when the margins of income are above the minimum can foresight come into play. It was indeed the secure upper and middle classes of Europe's society and not the necessitous masses that started the trend toward reduced fertility. Not poverty and disease, but improved living conditions and rising aspirations motivated the trend toward birth regulation.

Malthus is important today as the father of the most regressive social doctrine of our time, and as an expositor of some fundamental principles of population. His truth lives, but under the cloud of his errors.

The point of view in the last two essays is entirely different from that of Malthus. He saw the difficulties, not mainly as problems to be solved, but as the wise dispositions of the Creator to inculcate prudential restraint. The virtue was restraint; the reward was happiness in this world and the next. Huxley and Osborn see the regulation of fertility, not as a virtue in its own right, but as a means of bringing man into equilibrium with his environment. Under these circumstances, technical advances can be used, not merely to support more people, but to bring the whole human race to new levels of health, education and freedom from want.

Huxley's brief statement stresses the need for coming into equilibrium with the physical and biological environment, and the roles that birth control and world-wide responsibility in conservation and economic development can play. Osborn's more extended summary goes on to consider the difficult problem of creating an awareness of the need for reduced fertility and the way in which the modern West can help a religiously, politically, and ethnically sensitive world achieve lower fertility. In the hands of these writers, the analysis of population growth is no longer an excuse for inaction on the part of the prosperous. It is instead a clear statement of universal responsibility in helping mankind attain both the understanding and the means of achieving the elemental prerequisites of the good life.

FRANK W. NOTESTEIN
President
The Population Council

THOMAS MALTHUS

• 1830 •

The following essay, entitled "A Summary View of the Principle of Population," was published in 1830, after having appeared in slightly longer form in the 1824 supplement to the *Encyclopaedia Britannica.*

IN TAKING a view of animated nature, we cannot fail to be struck with a prodigious power of increase in plants and animals. Their capacity in this respect is indeed almost infinitely various, according with the endless variety of the works of nature and the different purposes which they seem appointed to fulfil. But whether they increase slowly or rapidly, if they increase by seed or generation, their natural tendency must be to increase in a geometrical ratio, that is, by multiplication; and at whatever rate they are increasing during any one period, if no further obstacles be opposed to them, they must proceed in a geometrical progression.

In the growth of wheat, a vast quantity of seed is unavoidably lost. When it is dibbled instead of being sown in the common way, two pecks of seed wheat will yield as large a crop as two bushels, and thus quadruple the proportion of the return to the quantity of seed put into the ground. In *Philosophical Transactions* (1768) an account is given of an experiment in which, by separating the roots obtained from a single grain of wheat and transplanting them in a favourable soil, a return was obtained of above 500,000 grains. But without referring to peculiar instances or peculiar modes of cultivation, it is known that calculations have often been made, founded on positive experience of the produce of wheat in different soils and countries, cultivated in an ordinary way, and making allowance for all ordinary destruction of seed.

Humboldt has collected some estimates of this kind, from which it appears that France, the north of Germany, Poland, and Sweden, taken generally, produce from five to six grains for one; some fertile lands in France produce fifteen for one; and the good lands in Picardy and the Isle of France, from eight to ten grains for one. Hungary, Croatia, and Slavonia yield from eight to ten grains for one. In the Regno de la Plata, twelve grains for one are produced; near the city of Buenos Aires, sixteen for one:

in the northern part of Mexico, seventeen; and in the equinoctial regions of Mexico, twenty-four for one.[1]

Now, supposing that in any one country during a certain period and under the ordinary cultivation, the return of wheat was six grains for one, it would be strictly correct to say that wheat had the capacity of increasing in a geometrical ratio of such a nature as to sextuple itself every year. And it might safely be calculated hypothetically that if, setting out from the produce of one acre, land of the same quality could be prepared with sufficient rapidity and no wheat were consumed, the rate of increase would be such as completely to cover the whole earthy surface of our globe in fourteen years.

In the same manner, if it be found by experience that on land of a certain quality, and making allowance for the ordinary mortality and accidents, sheep will increase on an average so as to double their numbers every two years, it would be strictly correct to say that sheep have a natural capacity of increasing in a geometrical progression, of which the common multiple is two and the term two years; and it might safely be said that if land of the same quality could be provided with sufficient rapidity, and no sheep were consumed, the rate of increase would be such that if we were to begin with the full number which could be supported on an acre of land, the whole earthy part of the globe might be completely covered with sheep in less than seventy-six years.

If, out of this prodigious increase of food, the full support of mankind were deducted, supposing them to increase as fast as they have ever yet increased in any country, the deduction would be comparatively inconsiderable; and the rate of increase would still be enormous, till it was checked either by the natural want of will on the part of mankind to make efforts for the increase of food beyond what they could possibly consume, or, after a certain period, by their absolute want of power to prepare land of the same quality so as to allow of the same rate of progress.

Owing to these two causes combined, we see that notwithstanding this prodigious *power* of increase in vegetables and animals, their actual increase is extremely slow; and it is obvious that, owing to the latter cause alone, and

[1] *Essai Politique sur le Royaume de la Nouvelle Espagne,* IV, ix, 98.

long before a final stop was put to all further progress, their actual rate of increase must of necessity be very greatly retarded: it would be impossible for the most enlightened human efforts to make all the soil of the earth equal in fertility to the average quality of land now in use; furthermore the practicable approaches towards it would require so much time as to occasion at a very early period a constant and great check upon what their increase would be, if they could exert their natural powers.

Elevated as man is above all other animals by his intellectual faculties, it is not to be supposed that the physical laws to which he is subjected should be essentially different from those which are observed to prevail in other parts of animated nature. He may increase slower than most other animals, but food is equally necessary to his support; and if his natural capacity of increase be greater than can be permanently supplied with food from a limited territory, his increase must be constantly retarded by the difficulty of procuring the means of subsistence.

The main peculiarity which distinguishes man from other animals in the means of his support is the power which he possesses of very greatly increasing these means. But this power is obviously limited by the scarcity of land—by the great natural barrenness of a very large part of the surface of the earth—and by the decreasing proportion of produce which must necessarily be obtained from the continual additions of capital applied to land already in cultivation.

It is, however, specifically with this diminishing and limited power of increasing the produce of the soil that we must compare the natural power of mankind to increase in order to ascertain whether, in the progress to the full cultivation and peopling of the globe, the natural power of mankind to increase must not, of absolute necessity, be constantly retarded by the difficulty of procuring the means of subsistence; and if so, what are likely to be the effects of such a state of things.

In an endeavour to determine the natural power of mankind to increase as well as their power of increasing the produce of the soil, we can have no other guide than past experience.

The great check to the increase of plants and animals, we know from experience, is the want of room and nourishment; and this experience would direct us to look for the greatest actual increase of them in those situations where room and nourishment were the most abundant.

On the same principle, we should expect to find the greatest actual increase of population in those situations where, from the abundance of good land and the manner in which its produce is distributed, the largest quantity of the necessaries of life is actually awarded to the mass of the society.

Of the countries with which we are acquainted, the United States of America, formerly the North American Colonies of Great Britain, answer most nearly to this description. In the United States not only is there an abundance of good land, but from the manner in which it has been distributed and the market which has been opened for its produce, there has been a greater and more constant demand for labour, and a larger portion of necessaries has been awarded to the labourer than in any of those other countries which possess an equal or greater abundance of land and fertility of soil.

Here, then, we should expect to find that the natural power of mankind to increase, whatever it may be, would be most distinctly marked; and here, in consequence, it appears that the actual rate of the increase of population has been more rapid than in any known country, although, independently of the abundance of good land and the great demand for labour, it is distinguished by no other circumstances which appear to be peculiarly favourable to the increase of numbers.

It has been stated that all animals, according to the known laws by which they are produced, must have a capacity of increasing in a geometrical progression. And the question with regard to man is, what is the rate of this geometrical progression?

Fortunately in the country to which we should naturally turn our eyes for an exemplification of the most rapid rate of increase, there have been four enumerations of the people, each at the distance of ten years; and though the estimates of the increase of population in the North American Colonies at earlier periods were of sufficient authority, in the absence of more certain documents, to warrant most important inferences, yet as we now possess such documents, and as the period they involve is of sufficient length to establish the point in question, it is no longer necessary to refer to earlier times.

According to a regular census made by order of Congress in 1790, which there is every reason to think is essentially correct, the white population of the United States was found to be 3,164,148. By a similar census in 1800, it was found to have increased to 4,312,841. It had increased then during the ten years from 1790 to 1800 at a rate equal to 36.3 per cent, a rate which, if continued, would double the population in twenty-two years and about four months and a half.

According to a third census in 1810, the white population was found to be 5,862,092,[2] which, compared with the population of 1800, gives an increase in the second ten years at the rate of nearly 36 per cent, which, if continued, would double the population in about twenty-two years and a half.

According to the fourth census in 1820, the white population was found to be 7,861,710,[3] which, compared with the population of 1810, gives an increase in the third ten years, at a rate per cent of 34.1, which, if continued, would double the population in twenty-three years and seven months.

If we compare the period of doubling according to the rate of increase in the most unfavourable ten years of this series with twenty-five years, we shall find the difference such as fully to cover all the increase of population which would have taken place from immigration, or the influx of strangers.

It appears from a reference to the most authentic documents which can be collected on both sides of the Atlantic that the emigration to the United States during the last thirty years, from 1790 to 1820, falls decidedly short of an average of 10,000 a year. Dr. Seybert, the best authority on the other side of the water, states that from 1790 to 1810 it could not have been so much as 6,000 a year. Our official accounts of the number of emigrants to the United States from England, Ireland, and Scotland during the ten years from 1812 to 1821, inclusive, give an average of less than 7,000, although the period includes the extraordinary years 1817 and 1818, in which the

[2] These numbers are taken from Dr. Seybert's *Statistical Annals*, p. 23.

[3] This number is taken from the American National Calendar for 1822, and has since been compared with the original census as published for the use of the members of Congress.

emigrations to the United States were much greater than they were ever known to be before or after, up to 1820. The official American accounts, as far as they go, which is only for two years from the 30th September, 1819, tend to confirm this average,[4] and allowing fully for the emigrants from other European countries, the general average will still be under 10,000.

A new mode has, however, lately been suggested[5] of estimating the amount of increase in any country derived from emigration. It has been justly stated that when a census is taken every ten years, and the population is distinguished into those above and those below ten years of age, all above ten years of age, exclusive of immigrants, must have existed in the census immediately preceding, and consequently, after having made a proper allowance for the mortality during these ten years, the excess above the remaining number must be attributed to immigration. If we had the means of estimating with accuracy the loss which would be sustained in America in ten years by a population not increased by additional births, this mode of estimating the amount of immigration would be unobjectionable, and often very useful.

But, unfortunately, the means are deficient. Even the annual mortality in the United States is not known. It was supposed by Dr. Price to be 1 in 50; by Mr. Barton, 1 in 45; and it is stated by Mr. Bristed in *America and Her Resources* that the annual deaths average throughout the United States 1 in 40, in the healthiest districts 1 in 56, and in the most unhealthy 1 in 35.

If, however, we could ascertain accurately the average annual mortality, we should still be unable to ascertain the amount of the loss in question, as, under any given law of mortality, it would depend so very much upon the rate at which the population was increasing. The truth of this observation will be placed in a striking light by the following short table, with which we have been favoured by a very able calculator, Mr. Milne, author of a well-known *Treatise on Annuities and Assurances*. It is constructed on the supposition that the population, in each case, is always subject to the same law of mortality as that

[4] American National Calendar for 1821, p. 237, and *North American Review*, October, 1822, p. 304.

[5] This mode was suggested by Mr. Booth in Mr. Godwin's *Inquiry Concerning Population.*

which prevailed in all Sweden and Finland during the five years ended with 1805, and that the number of births in the present year in each case is 10,000.

	The population constantly the same.	The population increasing, and having increased in geometrical progression for more than 100 years, so as to double itself every	
		50 years.	25 years.
Total population 10 years since ..	393,848	230,005	144,358
Total above 10 years of age now ..	320,495	195,566	126,176
Died during the term of 10 years out of those living at its commencement	73,353	34,439	18,182
Being one of	5.3692	6.6786	7.9396

We see from this table that, under the same law of mortality, the difference of loss sustained in ten years by a people not increased by fresh births would, in the three cases supposed of a stationary population, a population doubling in fifty years, and a population doubling in twenty-five years, be as 1 in 5.3692, 1 in 6.6786, and 1 in 7.9396; and that when the population is doubling itself in twenty-five years, the loss would be very little more than one-eighth.

But the censuses must be allowed to form a prima-facie evidence that the population of the United States has for some time been going on doubling itself in twenty-five years; and assuming this evidence to be true, which we are warranted in doing till better evidence is produced on the other side, it will appear that the amount of immigration, deduced from the rule here referred to, is less than 10,000 a year.

Thus the white population of the United States in 1800 was 4,312,841.[6] This population, without further accession of births, would in 1810 be diminished one-eighth, or reduced to 3,773,736. In 1810, the population above ten years of age was 3,845,389; and subtracting the former number from the latter, the difference, or amount of immigration, will be 71,653, or 7,165 a year.

Again, the white population of 1810 was 5,862,092,

[6] Seybert's *Statistical Annals*, p. 23.

which, diminished by one-eighth in ten years, would be 5,129,331. The population above ten years of age in 1820, was 5,235,940.[7] Subtracting the former from the latter, the difference, or amount of immigration, is 106,608 or 10,660 a year—showing, as we should expect, a greater amount of immigration from 1810 to 1820 than from 1800 to 1810, but even in the latter ten years, and including emigrations from Canada as well as all other countries, little exceeding 10,000.

Altogether, then, we can hardly err in defect if we allow 10,000 a year for the average increase from immigration during the twenty-five years from 1795 to 1820; and applying this number to the slowest period of increase, when the rate was such as to double the population in twenty-three years and seven months, it may be easily calculated that in the additional year and five months, a population of 5,862,000 would have increased to an amount much more than sufficient to cover an annual influx of 10,000 persons, with the increase from them at the same rate.

Such an increase from them, however, would not take place. It appears from an account in the National Calendar of the United States for the year 1821, that of the 7,001 persons who had arrived in America from the 30th of September, 1819, to the 30th of September, 1820, 1,959 only were females, and the rest, 5,042, were males,[8] a proportion, which, if it approaches towards representing the average, must very greatly reduce the number from which any increase ought to be calculated.

If, however, we omit these considerations, if we suppose a yearly emigration from Europe to America of 10,000 persons for the twenty-five years from 1795 to 1820, the greatest part of which time Europe was involved in a most extensive scene of warfare requiring all its population, and further, if we allow for an increase of all the emigrants during the *whole period* at the fullest rate, the remaining numbers will still be sufficient to show a doubling of the population in less than twenty-five years.

The white population of 1790 was 3,164,148. This

[7] American National Calendar for 1822, p. 246.

[8] The details for the next year were not then printed, but it is known that the whole number of passengers arriving in the United States was 10,722, of which 2,415 were from the United States, leaving 8,307 foreigners.—*American Review*, October, 1822, p. 304.

population, according to the rate at which it was increasing, would have amounted to about 3,694,100 in 1795; and supposing it to have just doubled itself in the twenty-five years from 1795 to 1820, the population in 1820 would have been 7,388,200. But the actual white population of 1820 appears, by the late census, to be 7,861,710, showing an excess of 473,510, whereas an emigration of 10,000 persons annually, with the increase from them at 3 per cent, a rate which would double a population in less than twenty-four years, would only amount to 364,592.

But the most striking confirmation of the censuses of the United States, and the most remarkable proof of the rate of increase being occasioned almost exclusively by procreation, have been furnished to us by Mr. Milne. In his work on *Annuities and Assurances,* which contains much valuable and interesting information on the subject of population, he had noticed the effects of the frequent pressure of want on the labouring classes of Sweden, which, by increasing the proportion of deaths, rendered the law of mortality so accurately observed in that country by Professors Wargentin and Nicander inapplicable to other countries more favourably circumstanced. But the law of mortality was observed to be gradually improving from the time that Dr. Price constructed his Swedish table; and the period from 1800 to the end of 1805 was so free from scarcities and epidemics, and the healthiness of the country had been further so much improved by the introduction of vaccination, that he justly thought the law of mortality, as observed during these five years, might suit countries where the condition of the people was known to be much better than it had generally been in Sweden. On these grounds he applied the Swedish law of mortality during the term mentioned to the hypothesis of a population which had been increasing by procreation in geometrical progression for more than a hundred years so as to double every twenty-five years. Assuming this population to be one million, he distributed it, according to such supposed law of mortality, into the different ages referred to in the American censuses, and then compared them with the same number of persons distributed according to the actual returns of the ages in the American censuses for the three periods of 1800, 1810, and 1820.

The results are as follows:

Distribution of a Population of 1,000,000 *Persons in the Under-mentioned Intervals of Age.*

	According to			
		United States.		
Between the Ages of	The Hypothesis.	Census of 1800.	Census of 1810.	Census of 1820.
0 & 10	337,592	334,556	344,024	333,995
10 & 16	145,583	154,898	156,345	154,913
16 & 26	186,222	185,046	189,227	198,114
26 & 45	213,013	205,289	190,461	191,139
45 & 100	117,590	120,211	119,943	121,839
0 & 100	1,000,000	1,000,000	1,000,000	1,000,000
Under 16	483,175	489,454	500,369	488,908
Above 16	516,825	510,546	499,631	511,092

The general resemblance in the distribution of the ages in the three different censuses to each other and to the hypothesis clearly proves—

First, that the distribution of the ages, in the different enumerations, must be made with some care, and may, therefore, be relied on as in the main correct.

Secondly, that the law of mortality assumed in the hypothesis cannot deviate essentially from the law of mortality which prevails in the United States.

Thirdly, that the actual structure of the American population differs very little from what it would be if it were increasing regularly from procreation only, in geometrical progression, so as to double itself every twenty-five years; and that we may therefore safely infer that it has been very little disturbed by immigration.

If to these proofs of the rapid increase of population which has actually taken place we add the consideration that this rate of increase is an average applying to a most extensive territory, some parts of which are known to be unhealthy; that some of the towns of the United States are now large; that many of the inhabitants must be engaged in unwholesome occupations and exposed to many of those checks to increase which prevail in other countries; and further, that in the western territories, where these checks do not occur, the rate of increase is more rapid than the general average, after making the fullest allowance for immigration—it must appear certain that the rate at which the population of the whole of the United States has actually increased for the last thirty years must fall very decidedly short of the actual capacity of mankind to increase under the most favourable circumstances.

The best proof that can be obtained of the capacity of mankind to increase at a certain rate is their having really increased at that rate. At the same time, if any peculiarly rapid increase which had appeared to take place in a particular country were quite unsupported by other evidence, we might be disposed to attribute it to error or accident, and might scarcely be justified in founding important conclusions upon it. But this is far from being the case in the present instance. The rate of increase which has at times taken place in other countries, under the operation of great and obvious checks to the progress of population, sufficiently shows what might be expected if these checks were removed.

The countries most resembling the United States of America are those territories of the New World which lately belonged to Spain. In abundance and fertility of soil they are indeed superior; but almost all the vices in the government of the mother country were introduced into her colonial possessions, and particularly that very unequal distribution of landed property which takes place under the feudal system. These evils, and the circumstance of a very large part of the population being Indians in a depressed state and inferior in industry and energy to Europeans, necessarily prevent that rapid increase of numbers which the abundance and fertility of the land would admit of. But it appears from the instructive and interesting account of New Spain, which M. Humboldt has not long since given to the public, that for the last half of the eighteenth century, the excess of the births above the deaths and the progress of the population have been very great. The following are the proportions of burials to baptisms in the registers of eleven villages, the details of which were communicated to M. Humboldt by the curates:

	Burials.	Baptisms.
Dolores	100	253
Singuilucan	100	234
Calymaya	100	202
Guanaxuato	100	201
St. Anne	100	195
Marsil	100	194
Queretaro	100	188
Axapuzco	100	157
Yguala	100	140
Malacatepec	100	130
Panuco	100	123

The mean proportion is 100 to 183.

But the proportion which M. Humboldt considers as best suited to the whole of the population is 100 to 170.

In some of the villages above mentioned, the proportion of the births to the population is extraordinarily great and the proportion of deaths very considerable, showing in a striking point of view the early marriages and early deaths of a tropical climate and the more rapid passing away of each generation.[9]

At Queretaro, it appears that the baptisms were to the population as 1 to 14, and the burials as 1 to 26.

At Guanaxuato, including the neighbouring mines of St. Anne and of Marsil, the baptisms were to the population as 1 to 15, and the burials as 1 to 29.

The general result from all the information which could be collected was that the proportion of births to the population for the whole of the kingdom of New Spain was as 1 to 17, and of the deaths as 1 to 30. These proportions of births to deaths, if they were continued, would double the population in twenty-seven and a half years.

M. Humboldt further observes that the information which he had collected respecting the proportions of the births to the deaths, and of these to the whole population, proves that if the order of nature were not interrupted by some extraordinary and disturbing causes, the population of New Spain ought to double itself every nineteen years.[10]

It is known, however, that these causes do occur in the actual state of things: consequently we cannot consider the actual rate of the increase of population in New Spain as greater than according to the former calculation. But a rate of increase such as to double the population in twenty-seven and a half years, in spite of all the obstacles enumerated by M. Humboldt, is very extraordinary. It is next to the increase of the United States, and greatly superior to any that can be found in Europe.

Yet in Europe, the tendency to increase is always very strongly marked, and the actual increase for periods of some length is sometimes much greater than could be

[9] The details which M. Humboldt has given of the population of New Spain are highly interesting, as they are the first of any consequence which the public has yet received of a tropical climate. The peculiarities which mark them are exactly of the kind which might have been expected, though the proportion of births is still greater than we could have ventured to suppose.

[10] *Essai Politique sur le Royaume de la Nouvelle Espagne,* II, iv, 330, *et seq.* Vol. I.

expected beforehand, considering the obstacles to be overcome.

It appears from Sussmilch[11] that the population of Prussia and Lithuania, after the great plague in 1709 and 1710, doubled itself in about forty-four years, from the excess of the births above the deaths enumerated in the registers.

In Russia, the whole population in 1763 was estimated by enumeration and calculation at twenty millions, and in 1796 at thirty-six millions.[12] This is a rate of increase which would occasion a doubling in less than forty-two years.

In 1695, the population of Ireland was estimated at 1,034,000. According to the late returns in 1821, it had increased to the prodigious amount of 6,801,827. This is an example of an actual increase for 125 years together at a rate which would double the population in about forty-five years; and this has taken place under the frequent pressure of great distress among the labouring classes of society and the practice of frequent and considerable emigration.

But for the proof of the power of population to increase under great obstacles of the preventive as well as of the positive kind, we need not go out of Great Britain. The rate of increase since our enumerations have commenced has been very remarkable for a country which was considered as well peopled before, and some of the details accompanying the returns tend strikingly to illustrate the principle of population.

The population of Great Britain according to the late enumerations was, in 1801, 10,942,646, and in 1811, 12,596,803.[13] This is a rate of increase during the ten years of rather above 15 per cent, a rate which, if continued, would double the population in between forty-nine and fifty years.

By the last enumeration of 1821, it appears that the population was 14,391,631[14] which, compared with the population of 1811, gives a rate of increase during the ten years of 14.25 per cent, a rate which would double the population in about fifty-two years.

According to these numbers, the rate of increase during

[11] *Gottliche Ordnung,* Vol. I. Table XXI.
[12] Tooke's *View of the Russian Empire,* II, 126.
[13] *Population Abstract* (1821), "Preliminary Observations," p. 8.
[14] *Population Abstract* (1821), "Preliminary Observations," p. 8.

the last ten years was slower than that of the first; but it appears from the excess of the number of males above females in the enumeration of 1811—so opposite to the state of the population in 1801 and 1821 when the females exceeded the males, particularly at the latter period—that of the large number added to the population for the army, navy, and registered merchant ships in 1811, a considerable proportion must have been foreigners. On this account, and on account of the further difficulty of knowing what part of this number might properly belong to Ireland, it has been proposed to estimate the percentage rate at which the population has increased in each of the ten years by the females only; and according to this mode of computation the population increased during the first period at the rate of 14.02 per cent, and during the second at the rate of 15.82. This last rate of increase would double the population in less than forty-eight years.

The only objection to this mode of computation is that it does not take into consideration the greater destruction of the males during the war. In 1801, the females exceeded the half of the population by 21,031, and in 1821 by 63,890, while, at the intermediate period, owing to the causes above mentioned, the females fell short of the half of the males by 35,685.

When, however, a proper distribution has been made of the army and navy among the resident population, and taking England and Wales alone, it appears that from 1801 to 1811 the population increased at the rate of 14.5 per cent, and from 1811 to 1821, at the rate of 16.3 per cent.[15] At the former of these rates, the period of doubling would be rather above fifty years, at the latter, under forty-six years, and taking the whole period, the time of doubling would be about forty-eight years. Yet in Great Britain there is a much larger proportion of the population living in towns and engaged in occupations considered as unhealthy than in any other known country of the same extent. There are also the best reasons for believing that in no other country of the same extent is there to be found so great a proportion of late marriages, or so great a proportion of persons remaining unmarried, as in Great Britain. And if, under these circumstances, a demand for labour and an increase of the funds for its maintenance

[15] *Population Abstract* (1821), "Preliminary Observations," p. 32.

could for twenty years together occasion such a rate of increase as, if continued, would double the population in forty-eight years and quadruple it in ninety-six years, it is in the highest degree probable that if the encouragements to marriage and the means of supporting a family were as great as in America, the period of doubling in Great Britain would not be more than twenty-five years, even in spite of her great towns and manufactories, and would be decidedly less if these obstacles were removed.

Taking, therefore, into consideration the actual rate of increase, which appears from the best documents to have taken place over a very large extent of country in the United States of America, very variously circumstanced as to healthiness and rapidity of progress; considering further the rate of increase which has taken place in New Spain, and also in many countries of Europe, where the means of supporting a family and other circumstances favourable to increase bear no comparison with those of the United States; and adverting particularly to the great increase of population which has taken place in this country during the last twenty years under the formidable obstacles to its progress which must press themselves upon the attention of the most careless observer, it must appear that the assumption of a rate of increase such as would double the population in twenty-five years as representing the natural progress of population, when not checked by the difficulty of procuring the means of subsistence or other peculiar causes of premature mortality, must be very decidedly within the truth.

It may be safely asserted, therefore, that population, when unchecked, increases in a geometrical progression of such a nature as to double itself every twenty-five years.[16]

It would be unquestionably desirable to have the means of comparing the natural rate of the increase of population when unchecked with the possible rate of the increase of food in a limited territory, such as that in which man is actually placed; but the latter estimate is much more difficult and uncertain than the former. If the rate of the increase of population at a particular period of some little extent can be ascertained with tolerable exactness,

[16] This statement, of course, refers to the general result, and not to each intermediate step of the progress. Practically, it would sometimes be slower and sometimes faster.

we have only to suppose the continuance of the same encouragements to marriage, the same facility of supporting a family, the same moral habits, with the same rate of mortality, and the increase of the population at the same rate after it had reached a thousand millions would be just as probable as at any intermediate and earlier period; but it is quite obvious that the increase of food in a limited space must proceed upon a principle totally different. It has been already stated that while land of good quality is in great abundance, the rate at which food might be made to increase would far exceed what is necessary to keep pace with the most rapid increase of population which the laws of nature in relation to human kind permit. But if society were so constituted as to give the fullest scope possible to the progress of cultivation and population, all such lands, and all lands of moderate quality, would soon be occupied; and when the future increase of the supply of food came to depend upon the taking of very poor land into cultivation, and the gradual and laborious improvement of the land already cultivated, the rate of the increase of food would certainly have a greater resemblance to a decreasing geometrical ratio than an increasing one. The yearly increment of food would, at any rate, have a constant tendency to diminish, and the amount of the increase of each successive ten years would probably be less than that of the preceding.

Practically, however, great uncertainty must take place. An unfavourable distribution of produce, by prematurely diminishing the demand for labour, might retard the increase of food at an early period in the same manner as if cultivation and population had been further advanced; while improvements in agriculture, accompanied by a greater demand for labour and produce, might for some time occasion a rapid increase of food and population at a later period in the same manner as if cultivation and population had been in an earlier stage of their progress. These variations, however, obviously arise from causes which do not impeach the general tendency of a continued increase of produce in a limited territory to diminish the power of its increase in future.

Under this certainty with regard to the general tendency, and uncertainty in reference to particular periods, it must be allowable, if it throws light on the subject, to make a supposition respecting the increase of food in a limited territory which, without pretending to accuracy, is clearly more favourable to the power of the soil to produce the means of subsistence for an increasing population than any experience which we have of its qualities will warrant.

If, setting out from a tolerably well-peopled country such as England, France, Italy, or Germany, we were to suppose that by great attention to agriculture, its produce could be permanently increased every twenty-five years by a quantity equal to that which it at present produces, it would be allowing a rate of increase decidedly beyond any probability of realization. The most sanguine cultivators could hardly expect that in the course of the next two hundred years each farm in this country on an average would produce eight times as much food as it produces at present, and still less that this rate of increase could continue so that each farm would produce twenty times as much as at present in five hundred years, and forty times as much in one thousand years. Yet this would be an arithmetical progression and would fall short, beyond all comparison, of the natural increase of population in a geometrical progression, according to which the inhabitants of any country in five hundred years, instead of increasing to twenty times, would increase to above a million times their present numbers.

It will be said, perhaps, that many parts of the earth are as yet very thinly peopled and, under proper management, would allow of a much more rapid increase of food than would be possible in the more fully inhabited states of Europe. This is unquestionably true. Some parts of the earth would no doubt be capable of producing food at such a rate as to keep pace for a few periods with an unrestricted increase of population. But to put this capacity fully into action is of all things the most difficult. If it is to be accomplished by the improvement of the actual inhabitants of the different parts of the earth in knowledge, in government, in industry, in arts, and in morals, it is scarcely possible to say how it ought to be commenced with the best prospect of success, or to form a conjecture as to the time in which it could be effected.

If it is to be accomplished by emigration from the more improved parts of the world, it is obvious that it must involve much war and extermination besides all the difficulties usually attendant upon new settlements in uncivilized countries; and these alone are so formidable, and for a long time so destructive that, combined with the unwillingness which people must always naturally feel to quit their own country, much distress would be suffered at home before relief would be sought for in emigration.

But supposing for a moment that the object could be fully accomplished—that is, supposing that the capacity of the earth to produce the necessaries of life could be put fully into action, and that they were distributed in the proportions most favourable for the growth of capital and the effective demand for labour—the increase of population, whether arising from the increase of the inhabitants of each country or from emigrants issuing from all those countries which were more advanced in cultivation, would be so rapid that in a period comparatively quite short, all the good lands would be occupied and the rate of the possible increase of food would be reduced much below the arithmetical ratio above supposed.

If merely during the short period which has elapsed since our Revolution of 1688 the population of the earth had increased at its natural rate when unchecked, supposing the number of people at that time to have been only 800 millions, all the land of the globe, without making allowance for deserts, forests, rocks, and lakes, would on an average be equally populous with England and Wales at present. This would be accomplished in five doublings, or 125 years; and one or two doublings more, or a period less than that which has elapsed since the beginning of the reign of James the First, would produce the same effect from the overflowings of the inhabitants of those countries where, owing to the further progress of cultivation, the soil had not the capacity of producing food so as to keep pace with the increase of an unrestricted population.

Whatever temporary and partial relief, therefore, may be derived from emigration by particular countries in the actual state of things, it is quite obvious that, considering the subject generally and largely, emigration may be fairly said not in any degree to touch the difficulty. And whether we exclude or include emigration—whether we refer to particular countries, or to the whole earth—the supposition of a future capacity in the soil to increase the necessaries of life every twenty-five years by a quantity equal to that which is at present produced must be decidedly beyond the truth.

But if the natural increase of population, when unchecked by the difficulty of procuring the means of subsistence or other peculiar causes, be such as to continue doubling its numbers in twenty-five years, and if the greatest increase of food which, for a continuance, could possibly take place on a limited territory like our earth in its present state, be at the most only such as would add every twenty-five years an amount equal to its present produce then it is quite clear that a powerful check on the increase of population must be almost constantly in action.

By the laws of nature man cannot live without food. Whatever may be the rate at which population would increase if unchecked, it never can actually increase in any country beyond the food necessary to support it. But by the laws of nature in respect to the powers of a limited territory, the additions which can be made in equal periods to the food which it produces must, after a short time, either be constantly decreasing, which is what would really take place or, at the very most, must remain stationary so as to increase the means of subsistence only in an arithmetical progression. Consequently, it follows necessarily that the average rate of the *actual* increase of population over the greatest part of the globe, obeying the same laws as the increase of food, must be totally of a different character from the rate at which it would increase if *unchecked.*

The great question, then, which remains to be considered, is the manner in which this constant and necessary check upon population practically operates.

If the soil of any extensive well-peopled country were equally divided amongst its inhabitants, the check would assume its most obvious and simple form. Perhaps each farm in the well-peopled countries of Europe might allow of one, or even two doublings, without much distress, but the absolute impossibility of going on at the same rate is too glaring to escape the most careless thinker. When, by extraordinary efforts, provision had been made for four times the number of persons which the land can support at present, what possible hope could there be of doubling the provision in the next twenty-five years?

Yet there is no reason whatever to suppose that anything besides the difficulty of procuring in adequate plenty the necessaries of life should either indispose this greater number of persons to marry early, or disable them from rearing in health the largest families. But this difficulty would of necessity occur, and its effect would be either to discourage early marriages, which would check the rate of increase by preventing the same proportion of births, or to render the children unhealthy from bad and insufficient nourishment, which would check the rate of increase by occasioning a greater proportion of deaths—or, what is most likely to happen, the rate of increase would be checked partly by the diminution of births and partly by the increase of mortality.

The first of these checks may, with propriety, be called the *preventive check* to population; the second, the *positive check;* and the absolute necessity of their operation in the case supposed is as certain and obvious as that man cannot live without food.

Taking a single farm only into consideration, no man would have the hardihood to assert that its produce could be made permanently to keep pace with a population increasing at such a rate as it is observed to do for twenty or thirty years together at particular times and in particular countries. He would, indeed, be compelled to acknowledge that if, with a view to allow for the most sanguine speculations, it has been supposed that the additions made to the necessaries produced by the soil in given times might remain constant, yet this rate of the increase of produce could not possibly be realized; and that if the capacity of the soil were at all times put properly into action, the additions to the produce would, after a short time and independently of new inventions, be constantly decreasing till, in no very long period, the exertions of an additional labourer would not produce his own subsistence.

But what is true in this respect in reference to a single farm must necessarily be true of the whole earth, from which the necessaries of life for the actual population are derived. And what would be true in respect to the checks to population if the soil of the earth were equally divided among the different families which inhabit it, must be true under the present unequal division of property and variety of occupations. Nothing but the confusion and indistinctness arising from the largeness of the subject could make persons deny in the case of an extensive territory, or the whole earth, what they could not fail to acknowledge in the case of a single farm which may be said fairly to represent it.

It may be expected, indeed, that in civilized and improved countries, the accumulation of capital, the division of labour, and the invention of machinery will extend the bounds of production; but we know from experience that the effects of these causes, which are quite astonishing in reference to some of the conveniencies and luxuries of life, are very much less efficient in producing an increase of food; and although the saving of labour and an improved system of husbandry may be the means of pushing cultivation upon much poorer lands than could otherwise be worked, yet the increased quantity of the necessaries of life so obtained can never be such as to supersede, for any length of time, the operation of the preventive and positive checks to population. And not only are these checks as absolutely necessary in civilized and improved countries as they would be if each family had a certain portion of land allotted to it, but they operate almost exactly in the same way. The distress which would obviously arise in the most simple state of society from the natural tendency of population to increase faster than the means of subsistence in a limited territory is brought home to the higher classes of an improved and populous country in the difficulty which they find in supporting their families in the same rank of life with themselves, and to the labouring classes, which form the great mass of society, in the insufficiency of the real wages of common labour to bring up a large family.

If in any country the yearly earnings of the commonest labourers determined, as they always will be, by the state of the demand and the supply of necessaries compared with labour, be not sufficient to bring up in health the largest families, one of the three things before stated must happen; either the prospect of this difficulty will prevent some and delay other marriages; or the diseases arising from bad nourishment will be introduced and the mortality be increased; or the progress of population will be retarded, partly by one cause, and partly by the other.

According to all past experience and the best observations which can be made on the motives which operate upon the human mind, there can be no well-founded hope of obtaining a large produce from the soil but under a system of private property. It seems perfectly visionary to suppose that any stimulus short of that which is excited in man by the desire of providing for himself and family and of bettering his condition in life, should operate on the mass of society with sufficient force and constancy to overcome the natural indolence of mankind. All the attempts which have been made since the commencement of authentic history to proceed upon a principle of common property have either been so insignificant that no inference can be drawn from them, or have been marked by the most signal failures; and the changes which have been effected in modern times by education do not seem to advance a single step towards making such a state of things more probable in future. We may, therefore, safely conclude that while man retains the same physical and moral constitution which he is observed to possess at present, no other than a system of private property stands the least chance of providing for such a large and increasing population as that which is to be found in many countries at present.

But though there is scarcely any conclusion which seems more completely established by experience than this, yet it is unquestionably true that the laws of private property, which are the grand stimulants to production, do themselves so limit it as always to make the actual produce of the earth fall very considerably short of the *power* of production. On a system of private property no adequate motive to the extension of cultivation can exist unless the returns are sufficient not only to pay the wages necessary to keep up the population, which at the least must include the support of a wife and two or three children, but also afford a profit on the capital which has been employed. This necessarily excludes from cultivation a considerable portion of land which might be made to bear corn. If it were possible to suppose that man might be adequately stimulated to labour under a system of common property, such land might be cultivated, and the production of food and the increase of population might go on till the soil absolutely refused to grow a single additional quarter, and the whole of the society was exclusively engaged in procuring the necessaries of life. But it is quite obvious that such a state of things would inevitably lead to the greatest degree of distress and degradation. And if a system of private property secures mankind from such evils, which it certainly does in a great degree by securing to a portion of the society the leisure necessary for the progress of the arts and sciences, it must be allowed that such a check to the increase of cultivation confers on society a most signal benefit.

But it must perhaps also be allowed that under a system of private property, cultivation is sometimes checked in a degree and at a period not required by the interest of society. And this is particularly likely to happen when the original divisions of land have been extremely unequal and the laws have not given sufficient facility to a better distribution of them. Under a system of private property, the only effectual demand for produce must come from the owners of property; and though it be true that the effectual demand of the society, whatever it may be, is best supplied under the most perfect system of liberty, yet it is not true that the tastes and wants of the effective demanders are always, and necessarily, the most favourable to the progress of national wealth. A taste for hunting and the preservation of game among the owners of the soil will, without fail, be supplied if things be allowed to take their natural course; but such a supply, from the manner in which it must be effected, would inevitably be most unfavourable to the increase of produce and population. In the same manner, the want of an adequate taste for the consumption of manufactured commodities among the possessors of surplus produce, if not fully compensated by a great desire for personal attendance, which it never is, would infallibly occasion a premature slackness in the demand for labour and produce, a premature fall of profits, and a premature check to cultivation.

It makes little difference in the actual rate of the increase of population, or the necessary existence of checks to it, whether that state of demand and supply which occasions an insufficiency of wages to the whole of the labouring classes be produced prematurely by a bad structure of society and an unfavourable distribution of wealth, or necessarily by the comparative exhaustion of the soil. The labourer feels the difficulty nearly in the same degree, and it must have nearly the same results, from whatever cause it arises; consequently, in every country with which we are acquainted where the yearly earnings of the labouring classes are not sufficient to bring up in health the largest families, it may be safely said that population is actually checked by the difficulty of procuring the means of subsistence. And, as we well know that ample wages, combined with full employment for all who choose to work, are extremely rare—and scarcely ever occur, except for a certain time, when the knowledge and industry of an old country is applied, under favourable circumstances, to a new one—it follows that the pressure arising from the difficulty of procuring subsistence is not to be considered as a remote one which will be felt only when the earth refuses to produce any more, but as one which not only actually exists at present over the greatest part of the globe, but, with few exceptions, has been almost constantly acting upon all the countries of which we have any account.

It is unquestionably true that in no country of the globe have the government, the distribution of property, and the habits of the people been such as to call forth in the most effective manner the resources of the soil. Consequently, if the most advantageous possible change in all these respects could be supposed at once to take place, it is certain that the demand for labour and the encouragement to production might be such as, for a short time in some countries and for rather a longer time in others, to lessen the operation of the checks to population which have been described. It is specifically this truth constantly obtruding itself upon our attention which is the great source of delusion on this subject and creates the belief that man could always produce from the soil much more than sufficient to support himself and family. In the actual state of things, this power has perhaps always been possessed. But for it we are indebted wholly to the ignorance and bad government of our ancestors. If they had properly called forth the resources of the soil, it is quite certain that we should now have but scanty means left of further increasing our food. If merely since the time of William the Conqueror all the nations of the earth had been well governed, and if the distribution of property and the habits both of the rich and the poor had been the most favourable to the demand for produce and labour, though the amount of food and population would have been prodigiously greater than at present, the means of diminishing the checks to population would unquestionably be less. That difficulty in procuring the necessaries of life which is now felt in the comparatively low wages of labour almost all over the world, and is occasioned partly by the necessary state of the soil and partly by a premature check to the demand for produce and labour, would then be felt in a greater degree and would less admit of any relaxation in the checks to population because it would be occasioned wholly and necessarily by the state of the soil.

It appears, then, that what may be called the proportionate amount of the necessary checks to population depends very little upon the efforts of man in the cultivation of the soil. If these efforts had been directed from the first in the most enlightened and efficient manner, the checks necessary to keep the population on a level with the means of subsistence, so far from being lightened, would, in all probability, be operating with greater force; and the condition of the labouring classes, so far as it depends on the facility of procuring the means of subsistence, instead of being improved, would, in all probability, be deteriorated.

It is to the laws of nature, therefore, and not to the conduct and institutions of man, that we are to attribute the necessity of a strong check on the natural increase of population.

But, though the laws of nature which determine the rate at which population would increase if unchecked and the very different rate at which the food required to support population could continue to increase in a limited territory, are undoubtedly the causes which render necessary the existence of some great and constant check to population, yet a vast mass of responsibility remains behind on man and the institutions of society.

In the first place, they are certainly responsible for the present scanty population of the earth. There are few large countries, however advanced in improvement, the population of which might not have been doubled or tripled, and there are many which might be ten, or even a hundred times as populous, and yet all the inhabitants be as well provided for as they are now, if the institutions of society and the moral habits of the people had been for some hundred years the most favourable to the increase of capital, and the demand for produce and labour.

Secondly, though man has but a trifling and temporary influence in altering the proportionate amount of the checks to population or the degree in which they press upon the actual numbers, yet he has a great and most extensive influence on their character and mode of operation.

It is not in superseding the necessity of checks to population in the progress of mankind to the full peopling of the earth (which may with truth be said to be a physical impossibility), but in directing these checks in such a way as to be the least prejudicial to the virtue and happiness of society, that government and human institutions produce their great effect. Here we know from constant experience that they have great power. Yet, even here it must be allowed that the power of government is rather indirect than direct, as the object to be attained depends mainly upon such a conduct on the part of individuals as can seldom be directly enforced by laws, though it may be powerfully influenced by them.

This will appear if we consider more particularly the nature of those checks which have been classed under the general heads of preventive and positive.

It will be found that they are all resolvable into *moral restraint, vice,* and *misery*. And if, from the laws of nature, some check to the increase of population be absolutely inevitable, and human institutions have any influence upon the extent to which each of these checks operates, a heavy responsibility will be incurred if all that influence, whether direct or indirect, be not exerted to diminish the amount of vice and misery.

Moral restraint, in application to the present subject, may be defined to be abstinence from marriage, either for a time or permanently, from prudential considerations, with a strictly moral conduct towards the sex in the interval. And this is the only mode of keeping population on a level with the means of subsistence which is perfectly consistent with virtue and happiness. All other checks, whether of the preventive or the positive kind, though they may greatly vary in degree, resolve themselves into some form of vice or misery.

The remaining checks of the preventive kind are the sort of intercourse which renders some of the women of large towns unprolific; a general corruption of morals with regard to the sex, which has a similar effect; unnatural passions and improper arts to prevent the consequences of irregular connections. These evidently come under the head of vice.

The positive checks to population include all the causes

which tend in any way prematurely to shorten the duration of human life, such as unwholesome occupations, severe labour and exposure to the seasons, bad and insufficient food and clothing arising from poverty, bad nursing of children, excesses of all kinds, great towns and manufactories, the whole train of common diseases and epidemics, wars, infanticide, plague, and famine. Of these positive checks, those which appear to arise from the laws of nature may be called exclusively misery; and those which we bring upon ourselves, such as wars, excesses of all kinds, and many others which it would be in our power to avoid, are of a mixed nature. They are brought upon us by vice, and their consequences are misery.

Some of these checks, in various combinations and operating with various force, are constantly in action in all the countries with which we are acquainted and form the immediate causes which keep the population on a level with the means of subsistence.

A view of these checks, in most of the countries of which we have the best accounts, was taken in the *Essay on Population*. The object was to trace in each country those checks which appeared to be most effective in repressing population; and to endeavour to answer the question generally, which had been applied particularly to New Holland by Captain Cook, namely, By what means is the population of this country kept down to the number which it can subsist?

It was hardly to be expected, however, that the general accounts of countries which are to be met with should contain a sufficient number of details of the kind required to enable us to ascertain what portion of the natural increase of population each individual check which could be traced had the power to overcome. In particular, it was not to be expected that any accounts could inform us of the degree in which moral restraint prevails, when taken in its strictest sense. It is necessary, therefore, to attend chiefly to the greater or smaller number of persons who remain unmarried or marry late; and the delay of marriage owing to the difficulty of providing for a family, when the degree of irregularity to which it may lead cannot be ascertained, may be usefully called the prudential restraint on marriage and population. And this will be found to be the chief mode in which the preventive check practically operates.

But if the preventive check to population—that check which can alone supersede great misery and mortality—operates chiefly by a prudential restraint on marriage, it will be obvious, as was before stated, that direct legislation cannot do much. Prudence cannot be enforced by laws without a great violation of natural liberty and a great risk of producing more evil than good. But still, the very great influence of a just and enlightened government and the perfect security of property in creating habits of prudence cannot for a moment be questioned. The principal causes and effects of these habits are thus stated in the *Principles of Political Economy,* iv, p. 250.

From real high wages, or the power of commanding a large portion of the necessaries of life, two very different results may follow; one, that of a rapid increase of population, in which case, the high wages are chiefly spent in the maintenance of large and frequent families; and the other, that of a decided improvement in the modes of subsistence, and the conveniencies and comforts enjoyed, without a proportionate acceleration in the rate of increase.

In looking to these different results, the causes of them will evidently appear to be the different habits existing among the people of different countries and at different times. In an inquiry into the causes of these different habits, we shall generally be able to trace those which produce the first result to all the circumstances which contribute to depress the lower classes of the people, which make them unable or unwilling to reason from the past to the future and ready to acquiesce for the sake of present gratification in a very low standard of comfort and respectability; and those which produce the second result, to all the circumstances which tend to elevate the character of the lower classes of society, which make them approach the nearest to beings who "look before and after," and who, consequently, cannot acquiesce patiently in the thought of depriving themselves and their children of the means of being respectable, virtuous, and happy.

Among the circumstances which contribute to the character first described, the most efficient will be found to be despotism, oppression, and ignorance; among those which contribute to the latter character, civil and political liberty, and education.

Of all the causes which tend to encourage prudential habits among the lower classes of society, the most essential is unquestionably civil liberty. No people can be much accustomed to form plans for the future who do not feel assured that their industrious exertions, while fair and honourable, will be allowed to have free scope; and that the property which they either possess or may acquire, will be secured to them by a known code of just laws impartially administered. But it has been found by experience that civil liberty cannot be permanently secured without political liberty. Consequently, political liberty becomes almost equally essential; and in addition to its being necessary in this point of view, its obvious tendency to teach the lower classes of society to respect themselves by obliging the higher classes to respect them, must contribute greatly to all the good effects of civil liberty.

With regard to education, it might certainly be made general under a bad form of government, and might be very deficient under one in other respects good; but it must be allowed that the chances, both with regard to its quality and its prevalence, are greatly in favour of the latter. Education alone could do little against insecurity of property; but it would powerfully assist all the favourable consequences to be expected from civil and political liberty, which could not indeed be considered as complete without it.

The varying prevalence of these habits owing to the causes above referred to, combined with the smaller or greater mortality occasioned by other customs and the varying effects of soil and climate, must necessarily produce great differences in different countries, and at different periods, in the character of the predominant checks to population and the force of each. And this inference, which inevitably follows from theory, is fully confirmed by experience.

It appears, for instance, from the accounts we have received of ancient nations and of the less civilized parts of the world, that war and violent diseases were the predominant checks to their population. The frequency of wars and the dreadful devastations of mankind occasioned by them, united with the plagues, famines, and mortal epidemics of which there are records, must have caused such a consumption of the human species that the exertion of the utmost power of increase must, in many cases, have been insufficient to supply it; and we see at once the source of those encouragements to marriage and efforts to increase population which, with inconsiderable exceptions, distinguished the legislation and general policy of ancient times. Yet there were some few men of more extended views who, when they were looking to the settlement of a society in a more improved state, were fully aware that under the most beautiful form of government which their imagination could conceive, the greatest poverty and distress might be felt from a too rapid increase of population. And the remedies which they proposed were strong and violent in proportion to the greatness of the evil which they apprehended. Even the practical legislators who encouraged marriage seemed to think that the supplies of children might sometimes follow too rapidly for the means of supporting them; and it appears to have been with a view to provide against this difficulty, and of preventing it from discouraging marriage, that they frequently sanctioned the inhuman practice of infanticide.

Under these circumstances, it is not to be supposed that the prudential restraint on marriage should have operated to any considerable extent. Except in a few cases where a general corruption of morals prevailed which might act as a preventive check of the most vicious kind, a large portion of the procreative power was called into action, the occasional redundancy from which was checked by violent causes. These causes will be found resolvable almost wholly into vice and misery, the first of which, and a large portion of the second, it is always in the power of man to avoid.

In a review of the checks to population in the different states of modern Europe, it appears that the positive checks to population have prevailed less, and the preventive checks more, than in ancient times, and in the more uncultivated parts of the world. The destruction occasioned by war has unquestionably abated, both on account of its occurring on the whole less frequently, and its ravages not being so fatal either to man or the means of his support as they were formerly. And although in the earlier periods of the history of modern Europe, plagues, famines, and mortal epidemics were not unfrequent, yet as civilization and improvement have advanced, both their frequency and their mortality have been greatly reduced, and in some countries they are now almost unknown. This diminution of the positive checks to population, as it has been certainly much greater in proportion than the actual increase of food and population, must necessarily have been accompanied by an increasing operation of the preventive checks; and probably it may be said with truth, that in almost all the more improved countries of modern Europe, the principal check which at present keeps the population down to the level of the actual means of subsistence is the prudential restraint on marriage.

Yet in comparing together the accounts and registers of the different countries of modern times, we shall still find a vast difference in the character and force of the checks which are mainly in action; and it is precisely in this point of view that these accounts afford the most important instruction. Some parts of Europe are yet in an unimproved state and are still subject to frequent plagues and mortal epidemics. In these countries, as might be expected, few traces are to be found of the prudential restraint on marriage. But even in improved countries the circumstances may be such as to occasion a great mortality. Large towns are known to be unfavourable to health, particularly to the health of young children; and the unwholesomeness of marshy situations may be such as in some cases to balance the principle of increase, even when nearly the whole of the procreative power is called into action (which is very seldom the case) in large towns.

Thus in the registers of twenty-two Dutch villages given by Sussmilch,[17] the mortality (occasioned, as may be supposed, chiefly by the natural unhealthiness of the country) was as high as 1 in 22 or 23, instead of the more common proportion of 1 in 35 or 40; and the marriages, instead of being in the more usual proportion to the population of 1 in about 108 or 112, were in the extraordinary high proportion of 1 in 64,[18] showing a most unusual frequency of marriage, while, on account of the great mortality, the number of inhabitants was nearly stationary and the births and deaths about equal.

On the other hand, in Norway, where the climate and modes of living seem to be extremely favourable to health and the mortality was only 1 in 48, the prudential restraint on marriage was called more than usually into action, and the marriages were only 1 in 130 of the population.[19]

These may be considered as extreme cases, but the same results in different degrees are observable in the registers of all countries; and it is particularly to be remarked that in those countries where registers of births, deaths, and

[17] *Gottliche Ordnung*, I, 128.

[18] This very large proportion of marriages could not all have been supplied from the births in the country, but must have been occasioned in part by the influx of strangers.

[19] *Essay on Population* (6th ed.), I, 260.

marriages have been kept for a considerable time, the progressive diminution of mortality occasioned by the introduction of habits more favourable to health, and the consequent diminution of plagues and mortal epidemics, have been accompanied by a smaller proportion of marriages and births. Sussmilch has given some striking instances of the gradual diminution in the proportion of the number of marriages during a part of the last century.[20]

In the town of Leipzig, in the year 1620, the annual marriages were to the population as 1 to 82; from the year 1741 to 1756, they were as 1 to 123.

In Augsburg, in 1510, the proportion of marriages to the population was 1 in 86; in 1750 as 1 to 120.

In Danzig, in the year 1705, the proportion was as 1 to 89; in 1745, as 1 to 118.

In the Dukedom of Magdeburg, in 1700, the proportion was as 1 to 87; from 1752 to 1755, as 1 to 125.

In the principality of Halberstadt, in 1690, the proportion was as 1 to 88; in 1756, as 1 to 112.

In the Dukedom of Cleves, in 1705, the proportion was 1 to 83; in 1755, 1 to 100.

In the Churmark of Brandenburg, in 1700, the proportion was 1 to 76;[21] in 1755, 1 to 108.

Instances of this kind are numerous, and they tend to show the dependence of the marriages on the deaths in all old countries. A greater mortality almost invariably produces a greater number of early marriages; and it must be equally certain that except where the means of subsistence can be adequately increased, a greater proportion of early marriages must occasion a greater mortality.

The proportion of yearly births to the whole population must evidently depend principally on the proportion of marriages and the age at which they are contracted; and it appears consequently from registers that in countries which will not admit of any considerable increase of population, the births and marriages are mainly influenced by the deaths. When an actual decrease of population is not taking place, the births will always supply the

[20] *Gottliche Ordnung,* I, 134, *et seq.*

[21] Some of these high proportions of marriages could not have taken place except under a shorter duration of human life, and a great proportion of second and third marriages, which have always a most powerful effect. In all considerable towns, also, the inhabitants of the neighbouring country increase the lists of marriages.

vacancies made by death, and exactly so much more as the increasing wealth of the country and the demand for labour will admit. Everywhere in the intervals of plagues, epidemics, and destructive wars, the births considerably exceed the deaths; but while from these and other causes the mortality in different countries is extremely various, it appears from registers that, with the allowance above stated, the births vary in the same proportion.[22]

Thus, in 39 villages of Holland, where the deaths at the time to which the registers refer were about 1 in 23, the births were also 1 in 23. In 15 villages around Paris, the births bore the same or even a greater proportion to the whole population on account of a still greater mortality, the births being 1 in 22.7 and the deaths the same. In the small towns of Brandenburg, which were in an increasing state, the mortality was 1 in 29, and the births 1 in 24.7. In Sweden, where the mortality was about 1 in 34.5, the births were 1 in 28. In 1,056 villages of Brandenburg, in which the mortality was about 1 in 39 or 40, the births were about 1 in 30. In Norway, where the mortality was 1 in 48, the births were 1 in 34.

Of all the countries reviewed in *The Essay on Population,* there is none which so strikingly illustrates the most important fact of the dependence of the proportions of marriages and births on the deaths, and the general principles of population, as Switzerland. It appears that between 1760 and 1770, an alarm prevailed respecting the continued depopulation of the country; and to ascertain the point, M. Muret, minister of Vevay, made a very laborious and careful search into the registers of different parishes, from the time of their first establishment. He compared the number of births which had taken place during three different periods of seventy years each, the first ending in 1620, the second in 1690, and the third in 1760. And finding by this comparison that the number of births was less in the second period than in the first, and less in the third period than in the second, he considered the evidence of a continued depopulation of the country from the year 1550 as incontrovertible.[23] But the accounts which he himself produces, clearly show that

[22] Sussmilch, *Gottliche Ordnung,* I, 225; *Essay on Population* (6th ed.), I, 331.

[23] *Mémoires, &c., par la Société Economique de Berne* (1776). pp. 15, *et seq.; Essay on Population* (6th ed.), I, 338, *et seq.*

in the earlier periods to which he refers, the mortality was very much greater than in the latter; and, that the greater *number* of births found in the registers formerly was not owing to a greater population but to the greater *proportion* of births which almost always accompanies a greater mortality.

It appears from accounts which are entirely to be depended on that during the last period, the mortality was extraordinarily small and the proportion of children reared from infancy to puberty extraordinarily great. At the time when M. Muret wrote his paper, in 1766, the proportion of deaths to the population in the Pays de Vaud was 1 in 45, of births 1 in 36, and of marriages 1 in 140. These are all very small proportions of births, deaths, and marriages compared with other countries; but the state of things must have been totally different in the sixteenth and seventeenth centuries. M. Muret gives a list of all the plagues which had prevailed in Switzerland from 1520, from which it appears that this dreadful scourge desolated the country at short intervals during the whole of the first period, and extended its occasional ravages to within twenty-two years of the termination of the second. We may safely conclude that in these times the average mortality was very much greater than at present. But what puts the question beyond a doubt is the great mortality which prevailed in the neighbouring town of Geneva in the sixteenth century, and its gradual diminution in the seventeenth and eighteenth. It appears from calculations published in the *Bibliothèque Britannique* (IV, 328), that in the sixteenth century, the probability of life, or the age to which half of the born lived, was only 4.883, or under four years and eleven months; and the mean life, or the average number of years due to each person 18.511, or about eighteen years and a half. In the seventeeth century, the probability of life in Geneva was 11.607, about eleven years and seven months; the mean life 23.358, or twenty-three years and four months. In the eighteenth century, the probability of life had increased to 27.183, twenty-seven years and two months; and the mean life to thirty-two years and two months.

There can be no doubt, from the prevalence of the plague and its gradual extinction as noticed by M. Muret, that a diminution of mortality of the same kind, though not perhaps to the same extent, must have taken place in

Switzerland; but if with a mortality which could not have been less than 1 in 30 or 32, the proportion of births had been what it was when M. Muret wrote, it is quite evident that the country would have been rapidly depopulated. But as it is known from the actual amount of births found in the registers that this was not the case, it follows as a necessary consequence that the greater mortality of former times was accompanied by a greater proportion of births. And this at once shows the error of attempting to determine the actual population, either of different countries or of different periods in the same country, by the amount of the births, and the strong tendency of population to fill up all vacancies, and very rarely to be limited by any other cause than the difficulty of supporting a family.

Switzerland and the Pays de Vaud afford other most striking instances of the dependence of the births on the deaths; and the accounts of them are perhaps more to be depended upon as they appear to contradict the preconceived opinions of the person who collected them.

Speaking of the want of fruitfulness in the Swiss women, M. Muret says that Prussia, Brandenburg, Sweden, France, and indeed every country the registers of which he had seen, give a greater proportion of baptisms to the number of inhabitants than the Pays de Vaud, where this proportion is only as 1 to 36. He adds that from calculations lately made in the Lyonnois, it appeared that in Lyons itself the proportion of baptisms was 1 in 28, in the small towns 1 in 25, and in the villages 1 in 23 or 24. What a prodigious difference, he exclaims, between the Lyonnois and the Pays de Vaud, where the most favourable proportion, and that only in two small parishes of extraordinary fecundity, is not above 1 in 26, and in many parishes it is considerably less than 1 in 40. The same difference, he remarks, takes place in the mean life. In the Lyonnois it is little above twenty-five years; while in the Pays de Vaud, the lowest mean life, and that only in a single marshy and unhealthy parish, is twenty-nine and one half years, and in many places it is above forty-five years.

"But whence comes it," he says, "that the country where children escape the best from the dangers of infancy, and where the mean life, in whatever way the calculation is made, is higher than in any other, should be precisely that in which the fecundity is the smallest?

How comes it again, that of all our parishes, the one which gives the mean life the highest, should also be the one where the tendency to increase is the smallest?"[24]

To resolve this question, M. Muret says, "I will hazard a conjecture, which, however, I give only as such. Is it not that, in order to maintain in all places a proper equilibrium of population, God has wisely ordered things in such a manner as that the force of life in each country should be in the inverse ratio of its fecundity? In fact, experience verifies my conjecture. Leyzin, a village in the Alps, with a population of 400 persons, produces but a little above 8 children a year. The Pays de Vaud, in general, in proportion to the same number of inhabitants, produces 11, and the Lyonnois 16. But if it happen that at the age of twenty years, the 8, the 11, and the 16 are reduced to the same number, it will appear that the force of life gives in one place what fecundity does in another. And thus the most healthy countries, having less fecundity, will not over-people themselves, and the unhealthy countries, by their extraordinary fecundity, will be able to sustain their population."

These facts and observations are full of the most important instruction and strikingly illustrate the principle of population. The three gradations in the proportion of births which are here so distinctly presented to our view, may be considered as representing that variety in the proportion of births which is known to take place in different countries and at different periods; and the practical question is whether, when this variety prevails without a proportionate difference in the rate of increase, which is almost universally the case, we are to suppose, with M. Muret, that a special providence is called into action to render women less prolific in healthy countries and where improved habits of cleanliness have banished plagues and mortal epidemics; or to suppose, as experience warrants, that the smaller mortality of healthy and improved countries is balanced by the greater prevalence of the prudential restraint on marriage and population.

The subject is seen with particular clearness in Switzerland on account of the population of some of the districts being stationary. The number of inhabitants on the Alps was supposed to have diminished. This was probably an

[24] *Mémoires, &c., par la Société Economique de Berne* (1776), pp. 48 *et seq.*

error; but it is not improbable that they should have remained stationary, or nearly so. There is no land so little capable of providing for an increasing population as mountainous pastures. When they have been once fully stocked with cattle, little more can be done; and if there be neither emigration to take off the superabundant numbers, nor manufactures wherewith to purchase an additional quantity of food, the deaths must equal the births.

This was the case with the Alpine parish of Leyzin before referred to, where for a period of thirty years the mortality and the proportion of births almost accurately kept pace with each other; and where, in consequence, if the positive checks to population had been unusually small, the preventive checks must have been unusually great. In the parish of Leyzin, according to M. Muret, the probability of life was as high as sixty-one years;[25] but it is obvious that this extraordinary degree of healthiness could not *possibly* have taken place under the actual circumstances of the parish with respect to the means of subsistence if it had not been accompanied by a proportionate action of the prudential restraint on marriage; and accordingly, the births were only 1 in 49, and the number of persons below 16 was only one quarter of the population.

There can be little doubt that in this case the extreme healthiness of the people, arising from their situation and employments, had more effect in producing the prudential check to population than the prudential check in producing the extreme healthiness; yet it is quite certain that they must constantly act and react upon each other, and that if, when the circumstances are such as to furnish no adequate means for the support of an increased population and no relief in emigration, the prudential check does not prevail, no degree of natural healthiness could prevent an excessive mortality. Yet to occasion such a mortality, a much greater degree of poverty and misery must have taken place than in districts less favourably circumstanced with regard to health; and we see at once the reason why, in countries of mountainous pasture, if there be no vent in emigration, the necessity of the prudential check should be more strongly forced on the attention of the

[25] *Mémoires, &c., par la Societé Economique de Berne* (1776), Table V, p. 65 of the Tables.

inhabitants, and should, in consequence, prevail to a greater degree.

Taking countries in general, there will necessarily be differences as to natural healthiness in all the gradations, from the most marshy habitable situations to the most pure and salubrious air. These differences will be further increased by the nature of the employments of the people, their habits of cleanliness, and their care in preventing the spread of epidemics. If in no country was there any difficulty in obtaining the means of subsistence, these different degrees of healthiness would make a great difference in the progress of population; and as there are many countries naturally more healthy than the United States of America, we should have instances of a more rapid increase than that which has there taken place. But as the actual progress of population is, with very few exceptions, determined by the relative difficulty of procuring the means of subsistence and not by the relative natural powers of increase, it is found by experience that except in extreme cases, the actual progress of population is little affected by unhealthiness or healthiness; but that these circumstances show themselves most powerfully in the character of the checks which keep the population down to the level of the means of subsistence, and occasion that sort of variety in the registers of different countries which was noticed in the instances mentioned by M. Muret.

The immediate cause of the increase of population is the excess of the births above the deaths; and the rate of increase, or the period of doubling, depends upon the proportion which the excess of the births above the deaths bears to the population.

The excess of births is occasioned by, and proportioned to, three causes: first, the prolificness of the marriages; secondly, the proportion of the born which lives to marry; and, thirdly, the earliness of these marriages compared with the expectation of life, or the shortness of a generation by marriage and birth compared with the passing away of a generation by death.

In order that the full power of increase should be called into action, all these circumstances must be favourable. The marriages must be prolific, owing to their being contracted early;[26] the proportion of the born living to marry must be great, owing both to the tendency to marriage, and the great proportion of births rising to the age of puberty; and the interval between the average age of marriage and the average age of death must be considerable, owing to the great healthiness of the country and the expectation of life being high. Probably these three causes, each operating with the greatest known force, have never yet been found combined. Even in the United States, though the two first causes operate very powerfully, the expectation of life and, consequently, the distance between the age of marriage and the average age of death is not so favourable as it might be. In general, however, the excess of births which each country can admit being very far short of the full power of increase, the causes above mentioned contribute to the required supply in very various proportions, according to the different circumstances and habits of each state.

One of the most interesting and useful points of view in which registers can be considered is in the proofs which they afford of the varying prevalence of the prudential check to marriage and population in different countries and places. It has been not an uncommon opinion, and has even been strongly expressed of late years although the subject has been much better understood than formerly, that the labouring classes of people, under the circumstances in which they are placed, cannot reasonably be expected to attend to prudential considerations in entering upon the marriage state. But that this opinion does them great injustice is not only obvious to common observation, by which we can scarcely fail to see that numbers delay marriage beyond the period when the passions most strongly prompt to it, but is proved by the registers of different countries, which clearly show either that a considerable number of persons of a marriageable age never marry, or that they marry comparatively late and that their marriages are consequently less prolific than if they had married earlier. As the prudential re-

[26] By *early* is not meant a premature age; but if women marry at 19 or 20, there cannot be a doubt that, on an average, they will have a greater number of births than if they had married at 28 or 30.

straint on marriage may take place in either of these ways, it may prevail nearly in the same degree with a different proportion of marriages to the whole population; and further, with the same proportion of marriages there may be a very different proportion of births and rate of increase. But on the supposition of the same natural prolificness in the women of most countries, the smallness of the proportion of births will generally indicate with tolerable correctness the degree in which the prudential check to population prevails, whether arising principally from late and consequently unprolific marriages, or from a large proportion of the population dying unmarried.[27]

We must refer, then, to the different proportions of births in different countries as the best criterion of the different degrees in which the prudential restraint on marriage operates. These proportions vary from about 1 in 36 to about 1 in 19, or even 17, in different countries, and in a much greater degree in different parishes or districts.

A particular parish in the Alps has already been mentioned where the births were only a forty-ninth part of the population; and it appears by the late returns of the parish registers of England and Wales, that the births in the county of Monmouth are only 1 in 47, and in Brecon, 1 in 53; which, after making ample allowance for omissions, would show the prevalence of the prudential restraint on marriage in a high degree.

If in any country all were to marry at twenty or twenty-one, the proportion of the births would probably be more than 1 in 19; and this result would be still more certain if the resources of the country could not support an accelerated rate of increase than if the means of subsistence were in the greatest abundance and the demand for labour as effectual as it has ever been in the United States. On the latter supposition, taking the births at one-nineteenth and the expectation of life the same as it is in England, the

27 It is impossible to form any judgment of the natural prolificness of women in different countries from the proportions of births to marriages in their registers, because those proportions are always prodigiously affected by the rate of increase, the number of second and third marriages, and the proportion of *late* marriages. The registers of a country might mark four births to a marriage, and yet the women who in country situations marry at twenty might have on an average seven or eight births.

effect would be to occasion a most rapid increase of population; and the period of doubling, instead of being about forty-six or forty-eight years, would be less than in America. On the other hand, if the resources of the country could not support a more rapid increase than that which has taken place in England and Wales during the ten years previous to the census of 1821, the effect would be a great diminution in the expectation of life. If the births were 1 in 19 instead of 1 in 30, the same rate of increase would take place as at present, if the annual mortality were increased to about 1 in 26.5; and in that case, the expectation of life would be reduced in the proportion of from 41; or, as is more probable, from above 45 [28] to less than 26. This is the kind of effect which must inevitably follow the absence of the prudential check to marriage and population; and it cannot be doubted that a considerable part of the premature mortality which is found to take place in all parts of the world is occasioned by it. The laws of nature, in application to man as a reasonable being, show no tendency to destroy half of the human race under the age of puberty. This is only done in very particular situations, or when the constant admonitions which these laws give to mankind are obstinately neglected.

It has been said that a tendency in mankind to increase at such a rate as would double the population in twenty-five years, and, if it had full scope, would fill the habitable globe with people in a comparatively short period, cannot be the law of nature, as the very different rate of increase which is actually found to take place must imply such an excessive degree of mortality and destruction of life as to be quite irreconcilable with actual facts and appearances. But the peculiar advantage of a law of increase in a geometrical progression is that though its power be absolutely immense if it be left unchecked, yet when this becomes impossible, it may be restrained by a comparatively moderate force. It can never, of course, happen that any considerable part of that prodigious increase which might be produced by an uninterrupted geometrical progression should exist and then be destroyed. The laws of nature which make food necessary to the life of man, as well as of plants and animals, prevent the continued

[28] This may be presumed from the small annual mortality in this country during the ten years from 1810 to 1820.

existence of an excess which cannot be supported, and thus either discourage the production of such an excess, or destroy it in the bud in such a way as to make it scarcely perceptible to a careless observer. It has been seen that in some countries of Europe where the actual progress of the population is slower than in many others, as in Switzerland and Norway, for instance, the mortality is considerably less. Here, then, the necessity of a greater check to the natural progress of population produces no increase of mortality. And it appears, farther, that even the degree of mortality which in each year would be sufficient to destroy that excess of births which would naturally be produced if all married young and all could be supported, might take place, and often does take place in particular situations, and yet is very little noticed. About the middle of last century, the mortality of Stockholm and London was about 1 in 19 or 20. This is a degree of mortality which would probably keep the births on a level with the deaths even though all married at twenty. And yet numbers resorted both to Stockholm and London from choice, the greater part probably not aware that by so doing, they would shorten their own lives and those of their children, and the rest thinking that the difference was not worth attending to, or was at least balanced by the advantages of society and employment which the town presented. There is nothing, therefore, in the actual state of the mortality observed to take place in different countries and situations which, in the slightest degree, contradicts the supposition of a natural tendency to increase quite as great as that which has been stated.

It has been further remarked that as, in point of fact, it very rarely happens that mankind continue to increase in a geometrical progression of any kind, and only in a single instance in such a one as to double the population in twenty-five years, it is useless and absurd to lay any stress upon tendencies which never, for any length of time together, produce their natural effects. But it might really as well be said that we are not to estimate the natural rate of increase in wheat or sheep, as it is quite certain that their natural tendency to increase has never practically continued to develop itself for so long a time together as that of mankind. Both as a physical, and even economical question, it is curious and desirable to know the natural law of increase which prevails among the most important plants and animals. In the same view, it must be still more interesting to know the natural law of increase with respect to man. It may be said, indeed with truth, that the actual appearances all around us—the varying rate of increase in different countries, its very slow progress, or stationary state in some, and its very rapid progress in others—must be a mass of anomalies, and quite contrary to the analogies of all the rest of animated nature, if the natural tendency of mankind to increase be not, at the least, as great as that which is developed under the most favourable circumstances, while in all others it is kept down by the varying difficulties which the state of the soil and other obstacles oppose to it. But the question as it applies to man assumes at once a tenfold importance in reference to the moral and political effects which must result from those checks to increase, the existence and operation of which, in some form or other, no human exertions can by possibility prevent. A field is here opened for the most interesting inquiries which can engage the friends of human happiness.

But as a preliminary to these inquiries, it is obvious that we must know the degree of force to be overcome, and the varying character of the checks which, in the different countries of the world, are practically found to overcome it; and, for this purpose, the first step must be an endeavour to ascertain the natural law of population, or the rate at which mankind would increase under the fewest known obstacles. Nor can this tendency to increase ever safely be lost sight of in the subsequent inquiries, which have for their object the improvement of the moral condition of man in society.

The existence of a tendency in mankind to increase, if unchecked, beyond the possibility of an adequate supply of food in a limited territory, must at once determine the question as to the natural right of the poor to full support in a state of society where the law of property is recognised. The question, therefore, resolves itself chiefly into a question relating to the necessity of those laws which establish and protect private property. It has been usual to consider the right of the strongest as the law of nature among mankind as well as among brutes; yet, in so doing, we at once give up the peculiar and distinctive superiority of man as a reasonable being and class him with the beasts of the field. In the same language, it may be said that the cultivation of the earth is not natural to man. It certainly is not to man, considered merely as an animal without reason. But to a reasonable being, able to look forward to consequences, the laws of nature dictate the cultivation of the earth, both as the means of affording better support to the individual and of increasing the supplies required for increasing numbers, the dictates of those laws of nature being thus evidently calculated to promote the general good and increase the mass of human happiness. It is precisely in the same way, and in order to attain the same object, that the laws of nature dictate to man the establishment of property and the absolute necessity of some power in the society capable of protecting it. So strongly have the laws of nature spoken this language to mankind and so fully has the force of it been felt, that nothing seems to be thought so absolutely intolerable to reasonable beings as the prevalence in the same society of the right of the strongest; and the history of all ages shows that if men see no other way of putting an end to it than by establishing arbitrary power in an individual, there is scarcely any degree of tyranny, oppression, and cruelty which they will not submit to from some single person and his satellites rather than be at the mercy of the first stronger man who may wish to possess himself of the fruit of their labour. The consequence of this universal and deeply seated feeling inevitably produced by the laws of nature, as applied to reasonable beings, is that the almost certain consequence of anarchy is despotism.

Allowing, then, distinctly, that the right of property is the creature of positive law, yet this law is so early and so imperiously forced on the attention of mankind that if it cannot be called a natural law, it must be considered as the most natural as well as the most necessary of all positive laws; and the foundation of this pre-eminence is its obvious tendency to promote the general good, and the obvious tendency of the absence of it to degrade mankind to the rank of brutes.

As property is the result of positive law, and the ground on which the law which establishes it rests is the promotion of the public good and the increase of human happiness, it follows that it may be modified by the same authority by which it was enacted, with a view to the more complete attainment of the objects which it has in view. It may be said, indeed, that every tax for the use of the government, and every county or parish rate, is a modification of this kind. But there is no modification of the law of property, having still for its object the increase of human happiness, which must not be defeated by the concession of a right of full support to all that might be born. It may be safely said, therefore, that the concession of such a right, and a right of property, are absolutely incompatible and cannot exist together.

To what extent assistance may be given, even by law, to the poorer classes of society when in distress without defeating the great object of the law of property, is essentially a different question. It depends mainly upon the feelings and habits of the labouring classes of society, and can only be determined by experience. If it be generally considered as so discreditable to receive parochial relief, that great exertions are made to avoid it, and few or none marry with a certain prospect of being obliged to have recourse to it, there is no doubt that those who were really in distress might be adequately assisted with little danger of a constantly increasing proportion of paupers; and, in that case, a great good would be attained without any proportionate evil to counterbalance it. But if, from the numbers of the dependent poor, the discredit of receiving relief is so diminished as to be practically disregarded, so that many marry with the almost certain prospect of becoming paupers, and the proportion of their numbers to the whole population is, in consequence, continually increasing, it is certain that the partial good attained must be much more than counterbalanced by the general deterioration in the condition of the great mass of the society and the prospect of its daily growing worse: so that, though from the inadequate relief which is in many cases granted, the manner in which it is conceded, and other counteracting causes, the operation of poor-laws such as they exist in England might be very different from the effects of a full concession of the right,[29] and a complete fulfilment of the duties resulting from it, yet such a state of things ought to give the most serious alarm to every friend to the happiness of society, and every effort consistent with

[29] The grand objection to the language used respecting the *right of the poor to support* is that, as a matter of fact, we do not perform what we promise, and the poor may justly accuse us of deceiving them.

justice and humanity ought to be made to remedy it. But whatever steps may be taken on this subject, it will be allowed that with any prospect of legislating for the poor with success, it is necessary to be fully aware of the natural tendency of the labouring classes of society to increase beyond the demand for their labour or the means of their adequate support, and the effect of this tendency to throw the greatest difficulties in the way of permanently improving their condition.

It would lead far beyond the limits which must be prescribed to this summary to notice the various objections which have been made by different writers to the principles which have been here explained. Those which contain in them the slightest degree of plausibility have been answered in the late editions of the *Essay on Population,* particularly in the appendix to the fifth and sixth, to which we refer the reader.[30] We will only, therefore, further notice the objection which has been made by some persons on religious grounds; for, as it is certainly of great importance that the answer which has been given to it should be kept in mind, we cannot refuse a place to a condensed statement of it at the end of this summary.

It has been thought that a tendency in mankind to increase beyond the greatest possible increase of food which could be produced in a limited space impeaches the goodness of the Deity, and is inconsistent with the letter and spirit of the Scriptures. If this objection were well founded, it would certainly be the most serious one which has been brought forwards; but the answer to it appears to be quite satisfactory, and it may be compressed into a very small compass.

[30] In the answer to Mr. Arthur Young, the question of giving land to cottagers is discussed; and it is a curious fact, that after proposing a plan of this kind, Mr. A. Young is obliged to own, "that it might be prudent to consider the misery to which the progressive population might be subject as an evil which it is absolutely and physically impossible to prevent." The whole of the difficulty, in fact, lies here. The grand distinction between colonies in England and Ireland and colonies in Canada is that in the one case there will be no demand for the progressive population from the colonists, and the redundancy of labour after a short time will be aggravated: in the other, the demand will be great and certain for a long time, and the redundancy in the emigrating countries essentially relieved.

The answer to Mr. Weyland, in the Appendix, contains much that is applicable to present objections.

First, it appears that the evils arising from the principle of population are exactly of the same kind as the evils arising from the excessive or irregular gratification of the human passions in general, and may equally be avoided by moral restraint. Consequently, there can be no more reason to conclude, from the existence of these evils, that the principle of increase is too strong than to conclude, from the existence of the vices arising from the human passions, that these passions are all too strong and require diminution or extinction instead of regulation and direction.

Secondly, it is almost universally acknowledged that both the letter and spirit of Revelation represent this world as a state of moral discipline and probation. But a state of moral discipline and probation cannot be a state of unmixed happiness, as it necessarily implies difficulties to be overcome and temptations to be resisted. Now, in the whole range of the laws of nature, not one can be pointed out which so especially accords with this scriptural view of the state of man on earth, as it gives rise to a greater variety of situations and exertions than any other, and marks, in a more general and stronger manner, and nationally as well as individually, the different effects of virtue and vice—of the proper government of the passions, and the culpable indulgence of them. It follows, then, that the principle of population, instead of being inconsistent with Revelation, must be considered as affording strong additional proofs of its truth.

Lastly, it will be acknowledged that in a state of probation, those laws seem best to accord with the views of a benevolent Creator, which, while they furnish the difficulties and temptations which form the essence of such a state, are of such a nature as to reward those who overcome them with happiness in this life as well as in the next. But the law of population answers particularly to this description. Each individual has, to a great degree, the power of avoiding the evil consequences to himself and society resulting from it, by the practice of a virtue dictated to him by the light of nature and sanctioned by revealed religion. And, as there can be no question that this virtue tends greatly to improve the condition and increase the comforts both of the individuals who practice it, and through them, of the whole society, the ways of God to man with regard to this great law are completely vindicated.

JULIAN HUXLEY

• *1955* •

The following essay, prepared after an around-the-world trip in 1954, appeared under the title "World Population" in *Scientific American,* March, 1956. It appears here without alteration as originally written in 1955.

THE problem of population is the problem of our age. In the middle of the twentieth century anyone who travels around the world, as I have recently done, cannot fail to be struck by the signs of growing pressure of population upon the resources of our planet. The traveler is impressed by the sheer numbers of people, as in China; by the crowding of the land, as in Java; by the desperate attempts to control population increase, as in Japan and India; and at the same time by the erosion, deforestation, and destruction of wildlife almost everywhere. The experiences of travel merely highlight and illustrate a fact which for some time has been obtruding itself on the world's consciousness: that the increase of human numbers has initiated a new and critical phase in the history of our species.

This crisis was recognized by the holding of a Conference on World Population in Rome in 1954. Held under the aegis of the United Nations, the Conference was a milestone in history, for it was the first official international survey of the subject of human population as a whole. In 1949 the UN had convened a scientific conference on world resources at Lake Success. As Director General of UNESCO, invited to collaborate in this project, I had suggested that a survey of resources should be accompanied by a similar survey of the population which consumed the resources. I was told that there were technical, political, and religious difficulties. Eventually these difficulties were smoothed over; censuses were taken; and a conference on population was duly held in 1954. During the five years it took to arrange for a look at the problem the world population had increased by more than 130 million.

Let me begin by setting forth some of the facts—often surprising and sometimes alarming—which justify our calling the present a new and decisive phase in the history of mankind. The first fact is that the total world population has been increasing relentlessly, with only occasional minor setbacks, since before the dawn of history. The second fact is the enormous present size of the population—more than 2.5 billion. The third is the great annual increase: some 34 million people per year, nearly 4,000 per hour, more than one every second. The human race is adding to its numbers the equivalent of a good-sized town, more than 90,000 people, every day of the year. The fourth and most formidable fact is that the rate of increase itself is increasing. Population, as Thomas Malthus pointed out in 1798, tends to grow not arithmetically but geometrically—it increases by compound interest. Until well into the present century the compound rate of increase remained below 1 per cent per annum, but it has now reached 1.33 per cent per annum. What is more, this acceleration of increase shows no sign of slowing up, and it is safe to prophesy that it will continue to go up for at least several decades.

In short, the growth of human population on our planet has accelerated from a very slow beginning until it has now become an explosive process. Before the discovery of agriculture, about 6000 B.C., the total world population was probably less than 20 million. It did not pass the 100 million mark until after the time of the Old Kingdom of Egypt, and did not reach 500 million until the latter part of the seventeenth century. By the mid-eighteenth century it passed the billion mark, and in the 1920's it rose above two billion. That is to say, it doubled itself twice over in the period between 1650 and 1920. The first doubling took nearly two centuries, the second considerably less than one century. Now, at the present rate of acceleration, the population will have doubled itself again (from the 1920 figure) by the early 1980's—i.e., in the amazingly short space of sixty years.

Each major upward step in numbers followed some major discovery or invention—agriculture, the initiation of urban life and trade, the harnessing of nonhuman power, the technological revolution. During the present century the most decisive factor in increasing population has been of a different sort—the application of scientific medicine, or what we may call death control. In advanced countries death rates have been reduced from the traditional 35 or 40 per thousand to less than 10 per thousand. The average life span (life expectancy at birth) has been more than doubled in the Western world since the mid-nineteenth century. It now stands at about seventy years in Europe and North America, and the process of lengthening life has begun to get under way in Asian countries: in India, for example, the life expectancy at birth has risen within three decades from twenty to thirty-two years.

Population growth appears to pass through a series of stages. In the first stage both the birth rate and the death rate are high, and the population increases only slowly. In the second stage the death rate falls sharply but the birth rate stays high; the population therefore expands more or less explosively. In the third, the birth rate also falls sharply, so that the increase of population is slowed. Finally both the birth and the death rates stabilize at a low figure; thereafter the population will grow only slowly unless it is spurred by some new development, such as access to new food sources or a change in ideas and values.

In the Western world the reduction of the death rate came gradually, and its effect on population growth was buffered by factors which tended at the same time to reduce the birth rate—namely, a rising standard of living and industrialization, which made children no longer an economic asset.

Matters have been very different in the still underdeveloped countries of Asia. There death control has been introduced with startling speed. Ancient diseases have been brought under control or totally abolished in the space of a few decades or even a few years. Let me give one example. In England malaria took three centuries to disappear; in Ceylon it was virtually wiped out in less than half a decade, thanks to DDT and a well-organized campaign. As a result of this and other health measures, the death rate in Ceylon was reduced from 22 to 12 per thousand in seven years—a fall which took exactly ten times as long in England. But the Ceylon birth rate has not even begun to drop, and so the population is growing at the rate of 2.7 per cent per annum—about twice the highest rate ever experienced in Britain. If this rate of growth continues, the population of Ceylon will be doubled in thirty years.

Almost all the underdeveloped countries are now in this stage of explosive expansion. When we recall that rates of expansion of this order (2 to 3 per cent) are at work among more than half of the world's 2.5 billion inhabitants, we cannot but feel alarmed. If nothing is done to control this increase, mankind will drown in its own flood, or, if you prefer a different metaphor, man will turn into the cancer of the planet.

Malthus, a century and a half ago, alarmed the world by pointing out that population increase was pressing more and more insistently on food supply, and if unchecked would result in widespread misery and even starvation. In recent times, even as late as the 1930's, it had become customary to pooh-pooh Malthusian fears. The opening up of new land, coupled with the introduction of better agricultural methods, had allowed food production to keep up with population increase and in some areas even to outdistance it. During the nineteenth century and the early part of the twentieth, food production increased in more than arithmetical progression, contrary to the Malthusian formula. We now realize, however, that this spurt in food production cannot be expected to continue indefinitely: there is an inevitable limit to the rate at which it can be increased. Although Malthus' particular formulation was incorrect, it remains true that there is a fundamental difference between the increase of population, which is based on a geometrical or compound-interest growth mechanism, and the increase of food production, which is not.

There are still some optimists who proclaim that the situation will take care of itself, through industrialization and through the opening of new lands to cultivation, or that science will find a way out by improving food-production techniques, tapping the food resources of the oceans, and so on. These arguments seem plausible until we begin to look at matters quantitatively. To accelerate food production so that it can keep pace with human reproduction will take skill, great amounts of capital and, above all, time—time to clear tropical forests, construct huge dams and irrigation projects, drain swamps, start large-scale industrialization, give training in scientific methods, modernize systems of land tenure and, most difficult of all, change traditional habits and attitudes among the bulk of the people. And quite simply there is not enough skill or capital or time available. Population is always catching up with and outstripping increases in production. The fact is that an annual increase of 34 million mouths to be fed needs more food than can possibly go on being added to production year after year. The growth of population has reached such dimensions and speed that it cannot help winning in a straight race against production. The position is made worse by the fact that the race isn't a straight one. Production starts far behind scratch: according to the latest estimates of the World Health Organization, at least two-thirds of the world's people are undernourished. Production has to make good this huge deficiency as well as overtake the increase in human numbers.

Is there then no remedy? Of course there is. The remedy is to stop thinking in terms of a race between population and food production and to begin thinking in terms of a balance. We need a population policy.

The most dangerous period lies in the next thirty or forty years. If nothing is done to bring down the rate of human increase during that time, mankind will find itself living in a world exposed to disastrous miseries and charged with frustrations more explosive than any we can now envision.

Even primitive societies practice some form of population control—by infanticide or abortion or sexual abstinence or crude contraceptives. Since the invention of effective birth control methods in the nineteenth century, they have been very generally practiced in all Western countries. Their spread to other cultures has been retarded by various inhibitions—religious, ideological, economic, political. It is worth noting that one retarding factor in the past has been the reluctance of colonial powers to encourage birth control in their colonies, often out of fear that they might be considered to be seeking to use population control as a weapon against an "inferior" race.

Today the underdeveloped countries are making their own decisions; what is needed is a new and more rational view of the population problem everywhere. We must give up the false belief that mere increase in the number of human beings is necessarily desirable, and the despairing conclusion that rapid increase and its evils are inevitable. We must reject the idea that the quantity of human beings is of value apart from the quality of their lives.

Overpopulation—or, if you prefer, high population density—affects a great many other needs of mankind besides bread. Beyond his material requirements, man needs space and beauty, recreation and enjoyment. Excessive population can erode all these things. The rapid population increase has already created cities so big that they are beginning to defeat their own ends, producing discomfort and nervous strain and cutting off millions of people from any real contact or sense of unity with nature. Even in the less densely inhabited regions of the world open spaces are shrinking and the despoiling of nature is going on at an appalling rate. Wildlife is being exterminated; forests are being cut down, mountains gashed by hydroelectric projects, wildernesses plastered with mine shafts and tourist camps, fields and meadows stripped away for roads and airports. The pressure of population is also being translated into a flood of mass-produced goods which is washing over every corner of the globe, sapping native cultures and destroying traditional art and craftsmanship.

The space and the resources of our planet are limited. We must set aside some for our material needs and some for more ultimate satisfactions—the enjoyment of unspoiled nature and fine scenery, satisfying recreation, travel, and the preservation of varieties of human culture and of monuments of past achievement and ancient grandeur. And in order to arrive at a wise and purposeful allocation of our living space we must have a population policy which will permit the greatest human fulfillment.

If science can be applied to increase the rate of food production and to satisfy our other needs, it can and should also be applied to reduce the rate of people production. And for that, as for all scientific advance, we need both basic research and practical application. Basic research is needed not only on methods of birth control but also on attitudes toward family limitation and on population trends in different sections of the world. Once we have agreed on the need for a scientific population policy, the necessary studies and measures to be applied will surely follow. This does not mean that we should envisage a definite optimum population size for a given country or for the world as a whole. Indeed, to fix such a figure is probably impossible, and to use it as a definite target is certainly impracticable. For the time being our aim should be confined to reducing the over-rapid population growth which threatens to outstrip food supply. If we can do this, our descendants will be able to begin thinking of establishing a more or less stable level of population.

With these general observations as our guide, we can now get a clearer grasp of the population problems of individual countries. Since the end of World War II, we have seen a new phenomenon in the world's history. Two great and powerful nations, India and Japan, have officially adopted the policy of population control.

Japan I was unable to visit, but its demographic plight is so extreme and so illuminating that I shall take it first. Japan's 90 million people are crowded into an area only one and one-half times as large as the small British Isles. The country is so mountainous that it affords only one-seventh of an acre of cultivable land per head. And its population is increasing by more than 1 per cent per annum, so that within ten years it will easily overshoot the 100-million mark.

The Japanese are not well nourished: the average daily calorie intake is only 2,000. About one-fifth of this meager food supply must be imported, despite the fact that the Japanese have developed the highest rice yield per acre in Asia. Since the war lost them their empire, and the isolation of Communist China deprived them of their biggest market, the Japanese have been able to subsist only through aid given by the United States. As a recent report on World Population and Resources by the Political and Economic Planning (P.E.P.) organization in Britain says: "Japan is undoubtedly the most overpopulated great country there has ever been."

Realizing that no expansion of its industry and trade could possibly take care of a major increase in its population, the Japanese Government has embarked on a firm policy of population control. In Japan infanticide was widely practiced until some eighty years ago. As its first move after the recent war the Government turned to an almost equally desperate measure: it legalized and indeed encouraged abortion. The number of induced abortions rose from a quarter of a million in 1949 to well over a million in 1953. As was to be expected, the effects on the health of Japanese women were deplorable—and the annual percentage rate of population increase was still above the prewar level.

With these stark facts in mind, the Japanese Ministry

of Health's Institute of Population Problems in 1954 passed a strong resolution urging government encouragement of contraception. It proposed that birth control facilities be provided as part of the health services, that medical schools pursue research and include family planning in the curriculum, that doctors called upon to induce an abortion should be required to provide the woman with information about birth control for the future, and that national wage and taxation policies should be such as to avoid "encouraging large families."

Drastic though these recommendations are, they or something very like them are necessary, and it is much to be hoped that they will be speedily and thoroughly implemented. If they are successfully put into practice, they will not only save Japan from disaster but will provide valuable lessons for other countries.

India's problem is rather different. It is an immense country—the best part of a subcontinent—with large resources waiting to be developed. Its present rate of population increase is just under 1.33 per cent per annum —lower than that in the United States (which is 1.6 per cent, excluding immigration). Its immediate future is not quite as desperate as Japan's.

But India is still in the early expanding stage of the population cycle. Its death rate (now about 26 per thousand) has just begun to fall, and has a long way to go before it drops to that of advanced countries. Meanwhile its birth rate (about 40 per thousand according to the latest available figures) is well over double that in western Europe, and shows no signs of dropping. If the death rate is cut to the extent that the Ministry of Health expects, and if the birth rate remains at its present level, within a few years India's annual increase of population will be some eight million—equivalent to adding a new London each year!

Moreover, India's population even now is not far from the borders of starvation; it must increase its food production drastically to achieve the barest minimum of decent living for its people. Their average daily diet is a mere 1,590 calories. At least two-thirds of India's 380 million people are undernourished. Methods of cultivation and systems of land tenure are primitive and will need a painful and difficult process of improvement before they begin to satisfy modern requirements. Tradition, taboos, ignorance, and illiteracy are grave obstacles to progress. Comparatively little more land could fruitfully be brought into cultivation, and deforestation compels the people to burn cow manure as fuel, thus robbing the soil of fertilizer.

Above all, the mere size of the problem is formidable. Even at the present rather modest rate of increase, five million people are added each year.

The size of India's human flood was forcibly brought home to me in 1954 when I visited the ill-fated Kumbh-Mela of that year. This religious festival is held at the junction of the two great rivers, the Jumna and the Ganges, at Allahabad. The assembled pilgrims acquire merit and salvation by bathing in the rivers' sacred waters. Every twelfth year the festival is especially sacred, and the Kumbh-Mela of 1954 was uniquely important as being the first of these high points to occur after India's independence. One day of the festival is particularly auspicious and to bathe on that day is especially efficacious.

Pilgrims had converged from all over India—by train, by cart, and by foot. On the day we arrived, two and a half million people were encamped on the flats by the river, and three days later, on the great day of the festival, the number had grown to four and a half million! I shall never forget the spectacle of this enormous human ant heap, with its local condensations of crowds converging onto the temporary pontoon bridges over the Jumna to reach the sacred bathing grounds. A crowd of this magnitude makes a frightening and elemental impression: it seems so impersonal and so uncontrollable. This impression was all too tragically borne out three days later, when the crowd got out of hand and trampled four hundred of its helpless individual members to death.

Calcutta was another manifestation of India's mere bulk. The overgrowth of cities has been a constant accompaniment of the growth of population: the hypertrophy of Calcutta has been exceptionally rapid and severe. In 1941 the population of greater Calcutta was under three million; today it is nearly five million. Its appalling slums are crowded to the rooftops, and at night the pavements are strewn with an overflow of people who have nowhere else to sleep and are forced to share the streets with the miserable roaming cattle. This was impressed upon me on the evening of my first day in the city by a scene I shall never forget. In one of the busiest streets a man and a cow approached a traffic island from opposite angles and composed themselves for the night on either side of the traffic policeman.

The Government of the new, independent India born in 1947 showed a refreshing courage in grasping the formidable nettle of overpopulation. Recognizing that superabundance of people was one of the major obstacles to Indian prosperity and Indian progress, they made the control of population one of the aims of their first Five-Year Plan. The Census Commissioner of India, in his report on the 1951 census, put the problem in quantitative terms. Efforts to keep pace with the growth of population by increasing food production were bound to fail, he said, when the population passed 450 million. If, however, India could "reduce the incidence of improvident maternity to about 5 per cent," an increase of 24 million tons per year in agricultural productivity would be sufficient to feed the population and bring a "visible reduction of human suffering and promotion of human happiness."

The Indian Health Ministry has made grants for research on new contraceptives, for certain population studies, for training workers in the field of family planning and maternal and child welfare, for educating public opinion, and for assisting the family-planning ventures of state governments and voluntary organizations.

It is heartening that a great country like India should make population control part of its national policy. But it must be confessed that the effects are as yet exceedingly small, and that to an outside observer the execution of the policy seems rather halfhearted.

Let me take an example. The one large-scale experiment initiated by the Government itself has been a pilot study of the so-called rhythm method of birth control, which is notoriously unreliable, owing to the great variation among individual women, and even in the same woman at different times, in the monthly period of infertility. I had the opportunity of visiting the chief center of the experiment in a village near Mysore, and of interviewing the capable and attractive woman in charge, a Negro social scientist from the United States.

The results of the experiment were interesting. About three-quarters of the married women in the village said they would like to learn some method of limiting their families. After their individual cycles were studied each woman was given a kind of rosary, with different colored beads for "safe days" and "baby days." With this guidance a number of the women managed to avoid pregnancy during the ten months of the experiment. The social scientist in charge thought that about 20 per cent of Indian village families might learn to practice the rhythm method successfully. This was a maximum; in any widespread campaign the figure is much more likely to be 15 or 10 per cent. Thus the method would be quite inadequate to control population growth to any significant degree.

Methods used in Western countries are difficult to apply in India, partly because of the cost, partly because of the lack of privacy and hygienic facilities in the vast majority of Indian homes. In addition, there is the persistent influence of Gandhi. As he narrated in his autobiography, Gandhi indulged excessively in sexual pleasure after his marriage. As a result of his disgust at his own indulgence, and his dislike of anything he considered to be scientific materialism, he pronounced against all mechanical or chemical methods of birth control and solemnly recommended abstinence as the cure for India's population problem!

The ideal solution would be the discovery of what laymen (much to the annoyance and distress of the experts) persist in calling "the pill"—a cheap and harmless substance taken by mouth which would temporarily prevent conception, either by preventing ovulation or by rendering the egg unfertilizable. A number of promising substances are being investigated, including some extracts of plants used by primitive peoples. So far nothing safe and reliable has emerged. But our knowledge of reproductive physiology and of biochemistry has been so enormously increased in the last few decades that I would be willing to bet that a solution can be found. A large-scale concerted program of research is necessary, as it was for the atomic bomb. If we were willing to devote to the problem of controlling human reproduction a tenth of the money and scientific brain-power that we are devoting to the release of atomic energy, I would prophesy that we would have the answer within ten years, certainly within a generation.

One of the facts that prompted the Indian Government to undertake the task of reducing population increase was the ghastly recurrence of famine in 1952, when a major tragedy was averted only by large-scale importations and gifts of wheat and other foodstuffs from other countries. Famine will continue to recur in India so long as population is not brought down into a reasonable balance with the production of food.

The Government has made heroic efforts to increase food production, and for the first time in modern history India has now a surplus of home-grown food—at the meager-diet level. But this has been made possible by two good seasons of abundant rain; when the climatic cycle brings the bad years around again, as it inevitably will, hunger once more will stalk the land. The long-term prospect is blacker: if population goes on increasing by five millions or more a year, food production cannot possibly continue catching up with the mouths to be fed.

The Government is also devoting more and more attention to industrializing the country, both by small-scale village industries and by large-scale projects. However, while industrialization is highly desirable, it is chimerical to suppose that it alone can cope with India's food and population problem.

Indonesia, another country with an extraordinary population problem, contains the most densely populated large island in the world. Java has more than 50 million people on its 50,000 square miles—a density of population nearly twice that of highly industrialized Britain. Yet Java is almost entirely agricultural. Its cultivable land is very fertile, but there is less than two-fifths of an acre per head. And much of the land is devoted to exportable products, so that rice has to be imported to feed the people, even at the insufficient level of about 2,000 calories per day.

Java's already overcrowded population is increasing at a compound interest rate of at least 1.5 per cent per year. A simple answer seems at hand: the excess should be transferred to the large nearby Indonesian islands of Sumatra and Borneo, which are far less thickly populated. But this facile suggestion has proved to be quite impracticable. With considerable difficulty the Indonesian authorities had persuaded some Javanese to move to Sumatra, but many of these have not been able to stand the hardships of pioneering agriculture and have either returned to Java or settled into a depressed urban life on the Sumatra coast. The fact is the material resources and the skills needed to convert the dense equatorial forest of Sumatra and Borneo to agricultural production are not available. This is not to say that settlement should not be attempted. But resettlement of Java's population on the largest possible scale, plus other economic and political development, could not possibly cope with more than a part of Java's formidable annual surplus of people. Birth control also is necessary. Unfortunately there is no sign yet that the Indonesian Government recognizes this necessity.

Bali, whose population density (over 500 per square mile) is about half that of Java, grows just about enough rice to feed itself. However, if its population continues to grow at the present high rate it will seriously outstrip food production in two or at most three generations. Bali provides an extreme illustration of the erosion of a culture by world population pressure. The Balinese have a rich and vital cultural tradition in which beauty is woven into everyday living. Every aspect of life is marked by some celebration or embellished with some form of decoration. Every Balinese participates in some form of creative activity—music, dance, drama, carving, painting, or decoration. What is more, the tradition is not rigid, and the culture is a living and growing one, in which local and individual initiative are constantly introducing novelty and fresh variety. But the Balinese are afflicted with many preventable diseases; they are largely illiterate (though far from uncultured); their religion is now being undermined by the Christian missionaries who have at last been allowed to work in Bali; growing economic pressure forces them to take advantage of the flood of cheap mass-produced goods from Western technology; their mounting population demands some adaptation to modern industrial life if living standards are to be raised or even maintained, and this in turn is imposing a westernized system of compulsory education.

Most foreign residents prophesy that Bali's unique and vital culture is doomed, and will wither and die within ten or fifteen years. This may be overgloomy, but certainly it is in grave danger. We can only hope that the Indonesian Government will realize the value of this rich product of the centuries, and that UNESCO will justify the C in its name—C for Culture—and do all in its power to help. No one wants to keep the Balinese in a state of ill health and ignorance. Yet instead of being pushed by the well-meaning but ill-considered efforts of over-zealous missionaries and "scientific" experts to believe that their traditional culture is a symbol of backwardness, they could be encouraged to retain faith in the essential validity of their indigenous arts and ceremonials, and helped in the task of adapting them to modern standards. A traditional culture, like a wild species of animal or plant, is a living thing. If it is destroyed the world is poorer.

The situation of Siam, or Thailand as it is now officially called, is in some ways not dissimilar to that of Bali. It is in the fortunate position of producing enough rice not only to feed its own people but also to export a considerable amount to less favored countries. Its people are well fed and look cheerful. Thailand is proud of its past, and especially of the fact that it alone of Southeast Asian countries has never lost its independence. There is a traditional culture in which the bulk of the people are content to find fulfillment, though there is not so much active participation or artistic creation as in Bali. At the same time, Thailand is crowded with organizations and agencies, international and national, which are giving advice and assistance on every possible subject: health, education, agriculture, democracy, scientific development, administration, industry, fish ponds, and rural community life. As a result the traditional Siamese culture is being crushed or undercut.

Unless Thailand's birth rate falls along with the death rate, she will lose her proud distinction among Asian countries, and will become seriously overpopulated well before the end of the century. Thailand needs better co-ordination of her departments of government with the motley collection of foreign agencies, and an over-all plan which would take account of population and traditional culture as well as food production and industry, science and education.

Fiji is another island, with another problem. Its population of about a third of a million is made up of two separate populations, which at present are about equal in number—the indigenous Fijians and the immigrants from India (together with a handful of Europeans, Chinese, and others).

The history of the two populations is instructive. The native Fijian population numbered nearly 200,000 in 1850, had fallen to 150,000 when the islands were taken over by the British in 1874, and was steadily reduced by a succession of epidemics to a point well under 100,000 before health measures introduced by an alarmed administration reversed the decline. It is now around 140,000. Immigration from India started in 1879 and has continued to the present day. The Indian population outstripped the Fijian during World War II and has now passed 150,000. Since its rate of increase is well above that of the Fijians, Indians will in the space of two or three generations constitute a large majority unless present trends change.

The two groups are very different in physique, cultural background, interests, and work habits. The Fijians have the finest physique I have ever seen: they make good soldiers and wonderful athletes. But their athletic and warlike propensities have induced no great keenness for Western education, and a definite dislike of regular agricultural work. Indians largely man Fiji's sugar plantation economy. They make excellent laborers and small farmers and traders, and have a notable thirst for education. They have even started secondary schools on their own initiative and at their own expense.

There is little intermarriage between the two groups, and indeed little liking. The Indians tend to regard the Fijians as barbaric, while the Fijians (who still take a sneaking pride in their warlike and cannibal past) find the Indians effeminate and affect to despise their laborious way of life. However, there are now signs of a *rapprochement,* and some of the younger Fijians are realizing that they must change their attitude toward work and education if the Fijian community is not to lapse into a sort of living fossil, cushioned by the protective measures of the Colonial Government. Once this new attitude is realized in practice, and the Fijians accept Western standards more wholeheartedly, their death rate is bound to fall and their numbers to jump. Since the Indian rate of increase shows no signs of falling, a demographic crisis looms ahead. Fiji will become overpopulated within the lifetime of its younger inhabitants unless the Fijians and Indians alike are introduced to the necessity and desirability of family limitation. Unfortunately birth control is still taboo, or at least not publicly acceptable, in the British Colonial Office (and indeed in the governments of all other colonial powers). I can only hope that too much economic distress and social misery will not be required to force the action that present intelligent foresight could undertake—and could now undertake with much less difficulty than when the cohorts of the yet unborn have swelled the population to disastrous proportions.

Australia is a storm center of demographic controversy. She is a continent of close on three million square miles with only nine million human inhabitants. Yet she is committed to a "white Australia" policy, and admits no Asians or Africans as immigrants, though she is on Asia's back doorstep. The three great swarming countries of Asia—India, China, and Japan—have for decades been casting longing eyes on Australian space as a possible outlet for their surplus people; if the Axis powers had won the war, the Japanese undoubtedly would have established settlements in Australia on a large scale.

However, Australia's open spaces are, from the point of view of human occupation, largely a mirage. For an indefinite time its uninhabited areas will remain blanks on the world's map. Three-quarters of Australia is desert or semidesert. At the present time only 2.5 per cent of Australia's land is cultivated. It is true that big irrigation schemes are being planned, and that the discovery that much poor land could be enriched by adding trace elements is heartening the farmers and wine growers and herders. But heavy additions of fertilizers would also be needed, and these, like irrigation schemes, are expensive.

"Never" is a big word, but it looks as if much of the land can never be brought into cultivation. I was driven down from Darwin to Alice Springs—a thousand miles of increasingly sparse bush and increasingly stony and barren soil, miserable and for the most part intractable to human effort. The best estimates put 7.5 per cent as the maximum area of Australia's surface which can be brought into cultivation, and to achieve even this will demand great effort and great expenditures of capital.

Australia is underpopulated in the double sense that it could support a larger population and that a larger population would benefit its economy. How much larger is a question. Some say 50 million people, but this seems an over-optimistic estimate. A total of 25 or at most 30 millions seems more reasonable. And this would absorb less than one year's increase of Asia's population, less than five years of that of India alone. Furthermore, Australia already is hard put to it to keep up living standards in the face of its present rate of population growth, which is one of the highest in the world (about 2.5 per cent per annum), thanks to its policy of encouraging and assisting immigration from Europe. Thus the idea of Australia becoming an outlet for the spill-over of Asia is chimerical. The highest rate of human absorption possible without jeopardizing economic health could not take care of more than a small fraction of Asia's annual increase.

The white Australian policy remains as an affront to Asian sentiment. But this too has, in my opinion, strong arguments in its favor. Certainly it cannot and should not be justified on grounds of racial superiority or inferiority: there is no such thing. But it can be justified on cultural grounds. Cultural differences can create grave difficulties in national development. They often do so when cultural and racial differences are combined. A large minority group which clings to its own standards and its own cultural and racial distinctiveness inevitably stands in the way of national unity and creates all sorts of frictions. And if the immigrant group multiplies faster than the rest of the population, the problem is aggravated, as we have seen in Fiji.

It should be put on record that there is little color prejudice in Australia. For its aborigines—the only non-white permanent inhabitants of the continent—the watchword now is assimilation: they are gradually to be incorporated into the country's social and economic life. Australia is also admitting a number of Asians as students or trainees, and giving them a very friendly welcome. What Australia seeks to guard against is the creation of permanent racial-cultural minorities.

Such are some of the population problems of individual countries as I saw them in my tour of Asia and the Far East. The obverse of the population problem is the problem of resources, and I must say a word about the alarming differentials in consumption between different regions and nations. Even in food these are serious enough. The average daily diet in India (1,590 calories) is less than half that in countries such as the United States or Ireland. And between the more privileged classes of favored countries and the poorer ones of the underdeveloped countries the difference of course is much greater—nearly fourfold instead of twofold. When we come to other resources, the contrasts are still more startling. In the field of energy, the per capita consumption of the United States is double that of Britain and more than twenty times that of India. The United States consumes eighty times more iron per capita than India and nearly two and one-half times more newsprint per capita than Britain. It uses about two-thirds of all the world's production of oil.

As facts like these seep into the world's consciousness, they are bound to affect the world's conscience. Such inequalities appear intolerable. The privileged nations are beginning to experience a sense of shame. This guilty feeling finds a partial outlet in the various international schemes for technical and economic assistance to underdeveloped countries. But these schemes are not nearly bold or big enough. We need a world development plan on a scale at least ten times as big as all existing schemes put together—a joint enterprise in which all nations would feel they were participating and working toward a common goal. To achieve even the roughest of justice for all peoples, the favored nations of the world will have not merely to cough up a fraction of their surpluses but voluntarily to sacrifice some of their high standard of living. For their part the underdeveloped countries, to qualify for membership in the international development club, must be willing not only to pledge themselves to hard and intelligent work but also to restrict their population growth.

As I have emphasized, the crux of the problem lies in establishing a satisfactory balance between the world's resources and the population which uses the resources. The Political and Economic Planning report to which I have referred surveys in some detail the prospects of the world's main resources for the next twenty-five years. It concludes that so far as energy, minerals, and other inorganic raw materials are concerned, the total world requirements probably can be met during that period, and for energy the prospect continues reasonably bright up to the end of the twentieth century. But when it comes to food, a world deficiency "of appalling magnitude" already exists, and "supplying the necessary foodstuffs to feed the expected newcomers and also to bring about substantial and lasting improvement in the position of the many millions now underfed is likely to prove exceedingly difficult and increasingly precarious."

This forecast, it must be emphasized, applies to global consumption; when we take the position of individual countries into account, the situation appears even more serious. The trend is toward a widening of the already grotesque differences in consumption between the well-nourished and the undernourished regions of the world. For one thing, a rise in living standards in food-exporting countries is reducing the amount of food they have available for export; for example, Argentina is exporting less meat because its people are consuming more of its production.

Everything points to one conclusion. While every effort must be made to increase food production, to facilitate distribution, to conserve all conservable resources, and to shame the "have" nations into a fairer sharing of the good things of the world with the "have-nots," this alone cannot prevent disaster. Birth control also is necessary, on a world scale and as soon as possible.

Though I may seem to have painted the picture in gloomy colors, I would like to end on a key of hope. Just as the portentous threat of atomic warfare has brought humanity to its senses and seems likely to lead to the abandonment of all-out war as an instrument of national policy, so I would predict that the threat of overpopulation will prompt a reconsideration of values and lead eventually to a new value system for human living. But time presses. This year will add more than 34 million people to humanity's total, and certainly for two or three decades to come each successive year will add more. If nothing is done soon, world overpopulation will be a fact well before the end of the century, bringing with it an explosive cargo of misery and selfish struggle, frustration and increasingly desperate problems.

It has taken just one decade from Hiroshima for the world to face up resolutely to the implications of atomic war. Can we hope that it will take no more than a decade from the 1954 World Population Conference in Rome for the world to face up equally resolutely to the implications of world overpopulation?

FREDERICK OSBORN

• *1960* •

The following essay, summarizing the findings and reports of the Population Council, was published by the Princeton University Press, 1958, under the title "Population: An International Dilemma." It appears here as valid for early 1960.

Foreword

IN MAN'S past history growth of population has been associated with national power, periods of prosperity, and individual well-being. But today there are many areas in which a rapid increase in numbers threatens a reduction in levels of living for the mass of the people. More and more governments are faced with the dilemma whether to encourage population growth, though this might be to the disadvantage of their people in the long run, or to attempt the immensely difficult task of reducing births.

Under these circumstances, interest in population problems has recently become acute. Many people are trying to influence public opinion on the subject in their own and other countries. But there has been no common agreement on how population problems should be presented. Too often an exaggerated expression of views has made for controversy and misunderstanding.

In the spring of 1955 The Population Council joined with a number of interested persons in forming the so-called "Ad Hoc Committee" in the hope that it might be possible to develop a common understanding of how best to approach the problems of world population growth. The Committee has provided a meeting place for discussion. Its members have sought to find agreement as to the nature of population problems in the different areas of the world, and to assess various desirable lines of action.

The nucleus of the Committee consisted of eleven persons who have attended a series of meetings held from November 1955 through May 1957. They included two professional demographers, a physical scientist concerned with natural resources and their relation to populations, a Roman Catholic sociologist, a geneticist and publicist, the author of an important book on the depletion of resources, the director of an institution concerned with international education, a foundation executive, a recent president of the Planned Parenthood Federation, and the executives of The Population Council.

The trustees of The Population Council have kept in close touch with the work of the Committee and have been represented at each of its meetings. A total of twenty-three guest discussants have prepared papers and taken part in the discussion. They have included Protestant and Roman Catholic clergy working in the fields of sociology and family life, economists, and scientists and laymen experienced in technical assistance and economic development.

In organizing its discussions the Committee asked itself certain questions which it considered in successive meetings. In advance of each meeting original papers were prepared by specially qualified persons. The papers were then circulated, and provided the background for the discussion. The present statement is in effect a summary of these papers and of the discussions which took place in the meetings of the Committee.

In reducing the five hundred closely typed pages of the proceedings to a briefer form, it was not possible to convey the meaning of those who took part as fully or as correctly as they might have desired. The summary does not necessarily represent the individual opinions of those who took part, nor does it sufficiently reflect the wealth of factual and scientific material included in the background papers. The present statement is, therefore, signed in the name of the rapporteur. He must be held responsible for all errors of omission or commission, while freely acknowledging that the ideas presented, in general, and in many cases the actual words, are those of the competent men and women who took part in the meetings.

FREDERICK OSBORN, *Rapporteur*

One: Outline of Present Conditions

I. THE NEED FOR RATIONAL REGULATION OF BIRTHS IN THE MODERN WORLD

1. The Extension of Life

About 30 years of life lay ahead of an average infant born in ancient Egypt, Greece, or Rome. As recently as 1880, death rates in Massachusetts still allowed only about 40 years of life on the average to each infant. Today infants born in European and other economically advanced nations have life expectancies of about 70 years.

Advances in health and longevity have also been made recently in many countries where levels of living are still low. The death rate of Ceylon has been cut in half within the brief period since the end of World War II, and death rates in India, Malaya, Thailand and many other countries have been reduced by a third. Further advances in public health may be expected to bring further spectacular declines in mortality. If wars and famines can be avoided, we can reasonably assume that the average life ahead of all babies in the world a decade from now will be twice as great as that of infants in the most advanced countries of ancient times. Perhaps no other achievement of civilization has added so much to human happiness.

2. The Effect on Population Growth

A reduction of deaths at early ages has about the same effect on population as an increase of births; it tends to produce rapid rates of population growth. Even if birth rates begin to decline, they may remain higher than death rates for long periods of time. Thus the reduction in mortality may lead to rapid and long continued increases in the number of people. The growth of world population from 1650 to 1950 and the United Nations "medium" estimate of growth, 1950 to 1980, are shown in Chart I.

The demographic history of Sweden illustrates the European pattern of transition in the relation of births to deaths. Beginning early in the nineteenth century, the

CHART I

World Population Growth

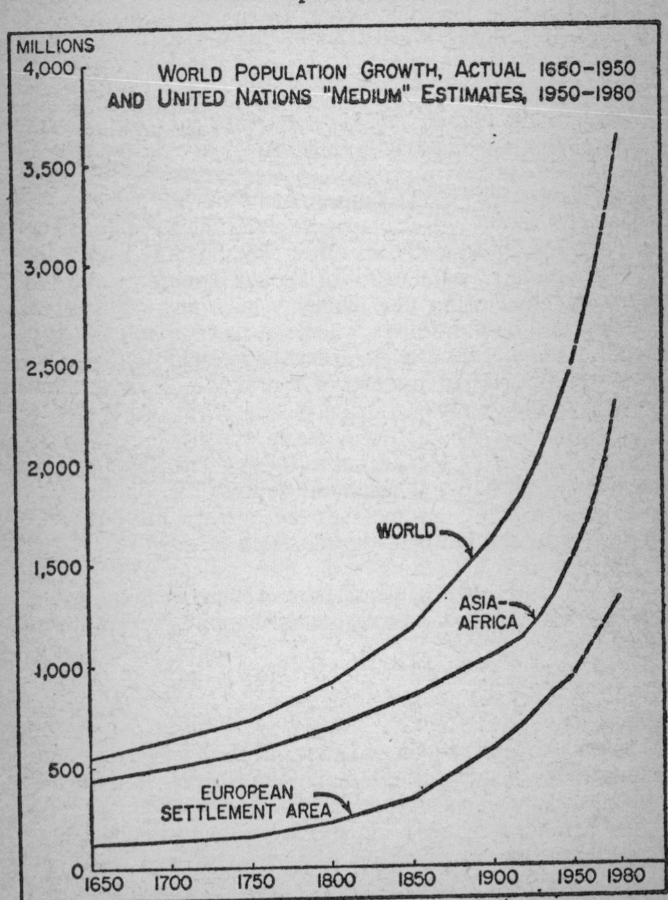

previous narrow margin between births and deaths widened and was freed from reversals caused by calamities. The gap remained wide and constant through the years from 1870 to 1900, with a large increase in population, while the birth rate declined. This was the first phase of the transition. Then early in the twentieth century the birth rate declined more rapidly than the death rate, and the gap was narrowed. Since then birth rates have been low and have fluctuated around a level only a little above the level of the low death rate. In this second phase of the transition the narrowing of the margin between births and deaths gave a new balance that was similar in its net effect on population growth to the old and costly balance obtained when more numerous births were offset by more numerous deaths. This was the second phase of the transition.

In Ceylon, the earlier phase of this transitional pattern was repeated, but much more suddenly. The reduction of deaths was brought about mainly by the application of new measures of public health through governmental and intergovernmental action, rather than through gradual changes in the habits of the people or their levels of living. Death rates dropped from 22 per thousand to 11 per thousand in less than a decade, without a corresponding decline in births. The latest information for Ceylon indicates an increase in population of about 2.8 per cent per year—much higher than rates of increase ever recorded in most European countries, and sufficient to more than double the population every twenty-five years. These two variations of the demographic transition in Sweden and in Ceylon are shown in Chart II.

In terms of general averages, European couples today average 2.3 children; couples in pre-modern Europe averaged about 5 children; and couples in most Asian countries average, even now, about 6 children. Fertility in some countries is much higher. Among the Armenians in the Transcaucasus and among settled Arabs in the Near East each woman has, on the average, about 8 children. One hundred and fifty years ago American women were having almost as many, with 7 or 8 on the average.

In advanced countries, the loss of reproductive force through the death of children at early ages is today almost negligible. For example, according to recent life tables for the Netherlands, 94.8 per cent of all females born alive live to have a thirtieth birthday. Under these conditions, if women exercised their full reproductive capacity, they would bear on the average well over 8 children for each woman living to the end of her reproductive period. Almost half of all infants are girls, and thus each woman would contribute, on the average, four potential mothers to the next generation. Since there are

CHART II

The Demographic Transition in Sweden and Ceylon

1: Vital Rates, Sweden, 1736-1953

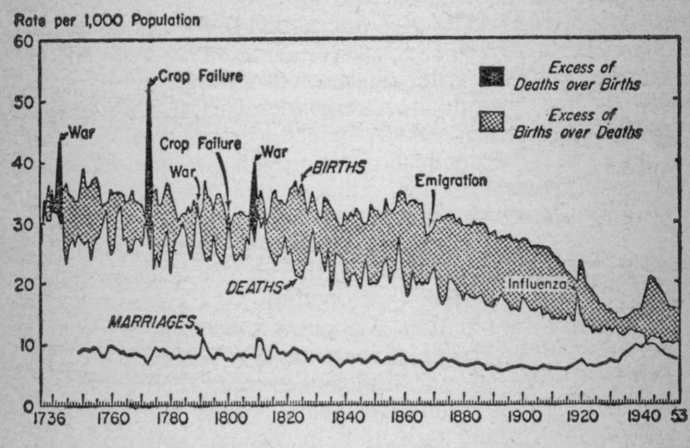

2: Vital Rates, Ceylon, 1900-1953

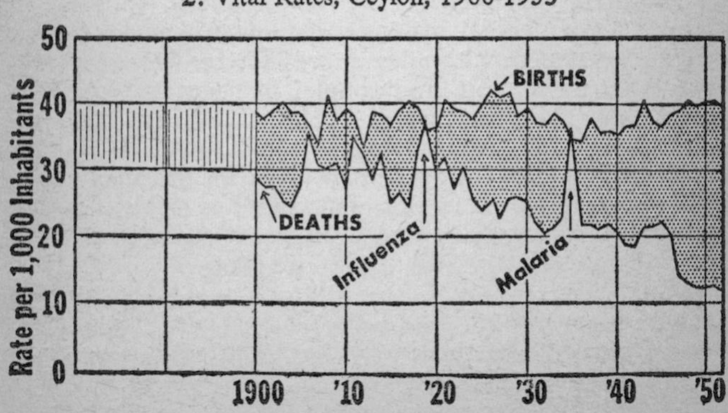

more than three generations in a hundred years, a completely unimpeded exercise of human reproductive capacity under modern conditions could give a 64-fold increase of population in less than a century (4 x 4 x 4 = 64). The continuation of early American fertility under present health conditions would have yielded an approximation of this trend. In fact, something of this sort is happening today in communities of the pious, rural Hutterites in the western United States and Canada.

Already in some countries the population is doubling in each generation of thirty years, involving an increase of about 2.5 per cent per year. And this rate of increase can be expected in other wide areas as death rates drop while birth rates remain very high. If continued, such growth would multiply the population eight times in less than a century and would bring a 64-fold increase in less than two centuries. It is not difficult to see that in any country, rich or poor, a continued increase of population at this rate must give rise to very formidable problems.

3. *Some Economic Effects of Too Rapid Growth*

One of the dangers facing nations that embark on new programs of economic development is that, although production may be gradually increased, the mounting needs of a rapidly increasing population may eat up part or all of these gains as fast as they are made—leading only to the sustenance of a larger population on the old level of poverty.

A recent study of economic trends in India came to the following conclusions, after taking into account the rapid advances in agriculture and manufacture which may be expected in the next thirty years. If there are continued declines in mortality but no decline in fertility, the population of India should reach 775 million by 1986, and by then consumption per consumer would be declining at the rate of 1 per cent per annum. If the declining mortality were accompanied by a 50 per cent decline in fertility between 1956 and 1981, the population of India would reach 590 million by 1986, and average per-consumer consumption would be 60 per cent higher than that attained under the high fertility assumption and rising at the rate of 4 per cent per annum.

It would be very hard to continue a stable, democratic government in India, or in any other country, if poverty and hunger were on the increase. The hopes of all mankind for orderly progress in a peaceful world may well depend in part on real achievements in bringing births into better balance with a reduced mortality.

In addition to its effect on gross rate of increase and size of population, the high birth rate characteristic of underdeveloped countries makes for many children relative to the number of adults. In a population with about 40 births per 1,000 persons each year, the ratio of children under 16 years of age to older persons will be in the vicinity of 40:60, rather than in the vicinity of 25:75 as in most Western nations where birth rates are 15 to 25 per 1,000. Obviously in the former case there are about twice as many children per adult as in the latter case.

The age structure of underdeveloped countries with high birth rates places an almost intolerable burden on families and communities. If the average investment of the underdeveloped countries in the nurture and development of each child absorbed a proportion of their income equal to that devoted to the rearing of children in the developed countries, the economic burden could not be met. The problem is usually solved by limiting the expenditure on each child to provision for his basic needs for food and other necessities. Even then children have to begin productive labor at an early age. Thus high fertility, through its effect on the rates of increase and age structure of populations, tends to impede national movements for promoting education and the acquisition of new skills.

4. The Effect of Excessively Large Families on Health and Family Life

In a primitive society with abundant resources the rearing of children may be relatively simple. The added burden of their food is soon offset by the contributions made by the children to the family living. There are no monetary cost requirements for their education, and the children are independent at an early age. The conditions of tribal and communal life ease the burdens of parents with large families. But recent studies indicate that in the primitive and impoverished areas of the world today few women want to have more than three or four children. The burden is too great.

The complex life of a more advanced society imposes new handicaps on parents of a large family. Children remain dependent on their parents through a longer period, perhaps until they are twenty or more. Education is an expensive matter, for the parents as well as for the community. New standards of infant and child care involve medical and advisory services at early ages, and all have to be paid for. The strain on the mother may be greater than it was under simpler conditions. Infant mortality is cut in half, but at a not inconsiderable expense in money, time, and nervous and emotional tension.

Whether in a primitive and low income area, or in an advanced society, raising a family makes heavy demands on the intelligence, the character, and the physical strength of the parents. Only the exceptional parents, and then only under exceptional conditions, can maintain high standards of family life, of child care and education, if they have more than four or five children. In such instances large families should be encouraged. But as a general rule it must be recognized that for most people in areas where birth rates are high and incomes are low, large families make it difficult to improve the care and education of children, and handicap all efforts to improve the quality of family life.

5. Special Problems of Countries Already Densely Populated

Other problems are encountered where large populations are dependent on relatively meager resources. In the first place, the accumulation of dense population on limited land resources is likely to have been achieved by reliance on techniques such as the cultivation of rice paddies with hand labor. This requires great expenditure of effort for small returns. But it may be impossible to change such practices without threatening the sustenance of the families and the nation's supply of food. Similarly, the development of plantations has supported great accumulations of population which are now dependent on the production of materials that must be exchanged in the world market, whether or not the terms are favorable. In fact, the outlook for some very dense populations in limited situations —for example in Haiti, Northern British Guiana, and East Pakistan—may be very dismal unless there are radical economic developments quite different in kind from those of the past.

Where population pressures on a limited amount of land result in intensive agricultural use of forested and mountain areas, or semi-arid grasslands, societies frequently deplete their land resources at rates likely to lead to disaster. Once such depletion of renewable resources and their bases has become a basis for the economy, it may become uneconomic if not virtually impossible to reverse the trend of depletion. Examples may be found in the past history of parts of Asia and the Middle East, and in the system of agriculture current today in Haiti and parts of Central and South America.

6. Some Special Problems of Advanced Countries

In economically advanced countries, fertility remains relatively high in families at the lowest levels of income and education. The most recent census data on this subject for the United States, the United Kingdom, and Sweden show the persistence of relatively high fertility among families with the most limited economic and educational resources. Excessive fertility by families with meager resources must be recognized as one of the potent forces in the perpetuation of slums, ill health, inadequate education, and even delinquency. A greater acceptance of the idea that parents should be responsible not to have more children than they can care for should go a long way toward improving this situation.

The characteristics of each new generation are, in part, determined by its origins. These include hereditary factors that are often transmitted with remarkable constancy through innumerable generations, and they include the cultural characteristics of the homes in which the children are reared. Differences of endowment by birth and by nurture profoundly influence the later personal lives of all men. More attention should, therefore, be given to the economic and social conditions which influence reproductive trends on human life in its qualitative aspects.

7. Summary

The attempt to control mortality is becoming a major social activity all over the world. The resulting decline in deaths is bringing about rapid changes in population trends. The rate of population growth in many underdeveloped areas is now much greater than was ever experienced in European countries. In most of the others it will be so in the foreseeable future. And the population base is far larger than it ever was in Europe. Unless an effort equal to that made for the control of death is made for the control of fertility, and unless a reduction of births is achieved within a few decades, the hopes of great but underdeveloped nations for better conditions of life may prove futile, while the present standard of economically advanced nations will decline. Such a tragic failure to achieve the higher levels of living that should be possible could only bring disillusion, confusion, and the danger of resort to desperate measures.

The rational planning of births is not an isolated process. It is not likely to come into play apart from progress along other lines. It does not compete with economic development. It is a complementary, not an alternative approach. Moreover, some economic progress may be made for a time in the face of uncontrolled fertility. But a rapid change to smaller planned families would in many countries vastly increase the efficiency of other constructive measures. The scale and tempo with which such a change occurs during the next few decades could well be the decisive factor in the race between progress and catastrophe in great nations that embrace a large share of humanity.

II. ATTITUDES AND PRACTICES AFFECTING FERTILITY

1. European Experience

The traditional social structure, the culture, and the historical development of western Europe enabled its population to enter the era of rapid technical advance with (1) a lower initial ratio of population to resources than many Asian nations possess today, (2) lower initial fertility, (3) a social structure amenable to entrepreneurial activity and social change. It also promoted (4) an approach to personal relations between men and women that may have influenced later trends in the control of fertility.

The folk culture of medieval Europe included many elements that limited the operation of values favorable to high fertility. Social conditions did not require universal marriage, or impel men and women to have children as early as possible, or provide rewards for large families. On the contrary, there were very considerable impediments against a realization of the full reproductive capacity of the population.

The primary unit in the social organization of European villages was the nuclear family, formed through the marriage of a man and a woman and including, as dependents, only their own children, along with any relatives deprived of support. This kind of family unit is in contrast to the extended or joint family common in Asian cultures. The emphasis on the nuclear family in Europe was in line with the individualistic legal and religious principles of late Hellenistic, late Hebraic, and early Christian cultures.

Each man at marriage became responsible for the support of his wife and of any children that might be born to them. It was commonly assumed that a man could not properly marry until he was in a position to discharge these responsibilities. Neither his parental family nor any larger kinship group regarded his children as their children or shared full responsibility for their nurture.

There was, in fact, strong social pressure against "improvident marriages." Sons who were assured of inheriting a living on the land were not encouraged to take wives while they were still young. Those who entered military orders had to postpone marriage, and those who entered religious orders had to forego marriage altogether. At the lower end of the social scale, servants and retainers were expected to remain single; there were often rules against the marriage of domestics. Edicts against the marriage of paupers were issued in many of the German states during the sixteenth and seventeenth centuries.

The economic pressure operating through this social system in medieval times was the limitation of land resources. The use of a plot of land of at least minimum size was needed to provide a living for each peasant family; and new lands could be brought into use only by slow degrees. At a later time, this pressure of limited resources gradually gave way to a desire for better houses, better clothing, better food, and the satisfaction of new interests which equally contributed to the postponement of marriage.

The average age of brides at first marriage in France in the late eighteenth century was about 25 years, and this average figure has remained fairly constant up to the last few years. Even around 1930, 38 per cent of all women aged 25 to 29 years old were still unmarried in the Netherlands, 41 per cent in England, 48 per cent in Switzerland, and 52 per cent in Norway—in contrast to 1 per cent in Korea, 2 per cent in India, 4 per cent in Formosa, and 8.5 per cent in Japan. The comparable figure for Ireland, in 1941, was 63.5 per cent.

Birth rates in Europe in the eighteenth century, prior to the commercial and industrial revolutions and the marked decline of fertility under modern conditions, were significantly lower than in most other parts of the world—not much above 30 per thousand in the Scandinavian countries, and between 30 and 40 per thousand throughout western Europe. A difference of 5 or 10 points per thousand is not striking in comparison with the wide variation in birth rates now found among various nations and among various classes within a nation. But, as death rates decline, such a difference in fertility has an important effect on rates of natural increase (determined by the excess of births over deaths).

In contrast to Asian cultures where there is little provision for intimate association outside the family between men and women in work and play, young men and women in Europe (except in the upper classes where maidens were zealously chaperoned) worked together in the fields and joined in village festivals during the long years between puberty and marriage. Many of these men and women became deeply attached to one another. But European culture firmly discouraged maternity out of wedlock. Even where community sentiments were relatively lax, the unmarried mother embarrassed her family and forced them to assume an unwelcome burden.

Community sentiment expected men to respect the interests of women; the men usually must have had some concern to protect women whom they loved from shame.

Thus through many centuries the European culture posed difficult problems in personal relations for couples deeply bound by emotional ties but unable to marry. They might at one extreme avoid all erotic association, or at the other ignore all inhibitions. Probably most chose some middle course. In this process it is possible that attempts to prevent conception became part of the European mores long before contraception was publicly advocated. The later acceptance of various forms of family limitation may thus have been made easier.

The emphasis in European culture on the nuclear family and the postponement of marriage for prudential reasons provided two possible approaches to a more drastic restriction of births, in response to new motivations. One possible approach was a tightening of the restraints on marriage. This approach was actually followed on a large scale in only one country: Ireland. The response was precipitated suddenly by the potato famine in 1845 and sustained by strong social and religious sentiments.

The alternative was the use of restrictive measures within marriage. This has been the preponderant response, beginning at different times, in all western European countries except Ireland. In the population of the United States contraceptive practices spread gradually, probably in advance of their spread through any country in Europe except France. Increase of contraceptive practice accompanied, step by step, the accelerated decline of fertility in the United States between 1890 and the 1930's.

Modern movements toward restriction of fertility in Europe were, in all cases, spontaneous personal responses under changing social conditions, wholly independent of governmental action. The support given to family limitation practices by organized institutions seems generally to have followed rather than to have initiated popular movements.

The family limitation movement in England was implemented at first mainly by an increased use within marriage of folk methods for preventing pregnancy. But we must not assume that family limitation could have gained the scope and force that it has attained in Europe, the United States, and some other regions, if the control of fertility had not been facilitated by new contraceptive techniques.

2. *Latin America*

In the relatively urban regions of southern South America, notably Uruguay and the Argentine, there have been declines in fertility similar to those in Canada and the United States. In Chile, also, there has been a substantial reduction in births.

The situation is quite different in northern South America, Central America, and the Caribbean. The people in these areas are largely agricultural, with low per capita incomes and widespread illiteracy. Most of the present populations were formed from the indigenous Indian population and immigrants from Spain or Portugal. In many areas there were substantial contributions from African slaves. Ancient cultural traditions, reinforced by Catholic teaching, have favored the persistence of high fertility. Recent improvements in public health have reduced mortality, and the average rate of natural increase is now as high or higher than in any other major world region. In Mexico, San Salvador, and some other areas where preventable diseases have been checked, the rate of natural increase per year may be 3 per cent or more.

In most of the countries which are the nearest southern neighbors of the United States, the economic aspects of population trends are very serious. And, due to cultural conditions, any incipient movements toward the control of population increase may encounter formidable obstacles.

Prospects for the reduction of population growth are much brighter in some Latin American countries outside of middle America. Although rapid population increase and various economic and cultural factors hamper the progress of capital formation, public education, and other progressive measures in Brazil and in Venezuela, the wealth of undeveloped resources in these countries and recent advances in industry should result in higher levels of living and other conditions tending to reduce births.

Any general statements about Latin America are dangerous. Conditions vary widely from country to country. There is, however, a trend toward greater regional and international cooperation in meeting common problems, including the need for statistical information and for scientific social studies. There are bright spots in the picture, but there are also very formidable problems.

3. The Caribbean

In another group of societies other patterns occur. In many parts of the Caribbean area "consensual marriages," in which there are no legal or religious obligations, are accepted as more or less equivalent to formal marriages. Such cultures are generally indifferent to fertility—without strong motivation for large families, but with no strong inhibitions against procreation. Formal or informal conjugal unions are established at early ages and, at least outside of the cities, there is little attempt to restrict fertility. Nevertheless, in some parts of the Caribbean, fertility is only moderately high, being checked to some extent by frequent estrangement between spouses, some involuntary sterility, and some resort to anti-natal practices.

Survey findings show wide popular interest in family limitation among Puerto Rican women. But in many areas Puerto Rican men consider that having many children is an index of their virility. Such an attitude encourages high fertility, particularly when, as in Puerto Rico, it is accompanied by lack of discussion between husband and wife. Interest in family limitation here appears to be positively associated with educational level, disapproval of consensual unions, approval of paid employment by women, and frequency of attendance at church; it is negatively associated with age and rural residence. Restriction of fertility within marriage, if effected at all, frequently involves sterilization. More than a tenth, perhaps a fifth, of all Puerto Rican mothers now arrange for sterilization after a third, fourth, fifth, or later child. The combination of favorable economic relations with the United States, opportunity for large-scale migration, and internal economic development, have brought a rapid rise of real incomes in Puerto Rico—along with some indications of a movement toward reduction in size of families.

4. Eastern and Southern Asia

In most Asian cultures the traditional family is in principle if not in fact an extended or joint family. Inheritance is patrilineal, and there is a strong emphasis on the unity of the paternal line through successive generations. These cultures prescribe the procreation and nurture of a son who must eventually assume his father's prerogatives; this is often a religious obligation. But there is no moral or religious prescription of unlimited fertility in any of these societies.

A common characteristic of social life in most Asian nations is early marriage. In some South Asian cultures, girls are married about the time of puberty, and child-bearing begins soon thereafter. It has been estimated that about 25 per cent of the potential reproductive capacity of women is eliminated by a prevention of pregnancies prior to twenty-five years of age. Thus the traditionally early marriage of women in South Asian societies has been conducive to high fertility.

In Asia at times when the problem of caring for children became critical, infanticide was probably the most widespread of all practices for limiting family size. Abortion too was widely used. Under primitive conditions abortion was a desperate measure. Yet both these grim expedients became sufficiently current in Japan during the century preceding the Meiji Reformation, when the trend toward increase of population brought misery and threatened disaster, to arrest the growth of population, as abortion has done again in the 1950's.

It is evident that a strong motivation for limitation of family size can bring about significant declines in fertility without any radical transformation of traditional social structure and values, whether Asian or European.

5. *The Modern Japanese Experience*

In Japan the national birth rate declined from about 35 per thousand in the early 1920's to about 30 per thousand in the middle 1930's. Three factors were involved in this decline, and they appear to have about equal weight: continued movement from rural areas, where fertility was relatively high, to cities; some raising of the ages of brides at marriage; and some extension of anti-natal practices within marriage.

After World War II the pressure of population in Japan was enormously increased. When the government made provisions for abortion available under respectable medical auspices and at low cost, the resort to abortions assumed the force of a mass movement. The number of reported abortions rose from 246,000 in 1949 to 1,068,000 in 1953. The total number of reported and unreported abortions in 1953 may have been larger than the total number (1,862,000) of live births. Meanwhile the birth rate had declined from 32.8 in 1949 to 21.5 per thousand in 1953. Since this time the birth rate has continued to decline to 18.4 per thousand in 1956, but apparently without any further increase in the frequency of abortion. This suggests a gradual shift toward reliance on contraception in the control of fertility.

Other more direct evidence indicates that the use of methods for preventing pregnancy was extended during this period. According to data from various surveys that are not wholly comparable, the proportions of couples with wives under fifty years of age reporting such practice rose from 15 per cent in 1949 to 28 per cent in 1952. According to a sampling survey of the total population carried out under the auspices of the Ministry of Welfare in April 1954, 33 per cent of all couples with wives under 50 years of age reported some previous contraceptive practice—37.2 per cent in urban areas, 30.4 per cent in rural areas. The proportion so reporting at this time rose from 21 per cent among wives under 20 years to 32 per cent at 20-24 years, and to 39 per cent at 25-29 years; it remained at about this level for wives 30-34 and 35-39 years, but declined sharply among older women. Only 10 per cent of wives aged 45-49 years reported that they had ever taken measures to prevent pregnancy. Among those reporting any contraceptive practice, 29 per cent had relied entirely on mechanical means, 20 per cent only on the safe period, and 13 per cent on a combination of these two methods, with the remainder divided between various other practices and combinations of practice.

It is important to note that in Japan the postwar movement to restrict fertility was felt to be consistent with firmly rooted loyalties to the family, the community, and the nation. In fact civic leaders in the nation and in its villages played a large role in promoting this movement—in contrast to the situation in Europe, or in Japan itself during the 1930's.

There is no justification for assuming that movements toward family limitation in most countries will necessarily run counter to established loyalties. On the contrary, established lines of group affiliation and leadership may, in some situations, become channels of positive influence in such movements.

6. The United States

Families in colonial America were generally larger than in Europe but a decline in the average number of children began in the United States earlier than in any European country except France. The decline continued throughout the nineteenth and into the twentieth century, and was sharply accelerated during the depression of the 1930's. This was a purely spontaneous movement in the face of a national tradition of growth, in the face of a general disapproval of family limitation by most religious bodies until quite recently, and in many states in the face of legal obstacles to the sale of contraceptives. The decrease has continued among very large families in the rural areas. But people are now marrying earlier, there are fewer childless couples and, especially among the more prosperous families, there seems to be an increasing regard for the values of family life, and a new emphasis on the desirability of moderately large families. It may be fair to say that in the main the people have regulated the size of their families in accord with their valuation of the good life for themselves and their children.

7. The Russian Experience

In the Soviet Union free medical services for abortion had been authorized soon after the Revolution and were gradually extended—along with a vigorous, but at first apparently ineffective, propaganda for contraception. The resort to the abortion clinics assumed mass proportions during the forced collectivization of agriculture, when there were civil wars in the countryside and food shortages in the cities, which resulted in a total loss by death of some five million persons more than would normally have been expected during the intercensus period, 1926-1939. In Moscow in 1934 there were 270 abortions per 100 births; and there were many abortions in the Ukraine and in Central Asia. The government, apparently alarmed at this trend, introduced restrictions in access to the abortion clinics in 1935, and closed them altogether in 1936—except for services on therapeutic or eugenic grounds. The birth rate which had dropped from about 45 in 1926-27 to about 30 in 1934-35 rose to 39 per thousand in 1937. It declined slightly in the following year, and has fallen to less than 25 per thousand at present. Many factors have contributed to the decline since 1937. They include increased education, industrialization and urbanization, and a shortage of housing, all accompanied by the spread of contraceptive practices.

8. *Concluding Observations*

Current generalizations about the effect on the birth rate of industrialization and education are largely based on European experience, including that of western European stocks in the new world and in Australia and New Zealand. It must be recognized that large proportions of the population of many undeveloped countries will remain in rural communities for many decades. Changes in size of family in these countries as a whole will, therefore, depend in large part on attitudes and practices in the villages. One cannot predict with confidence on the basis of European, or even of Soviet or Japanese experience, that spontaneous trends toward lower fertility will take place on a significant scale in most underdeveloped countries within the critical half-century that is opening before us. Neither is there any valid ground for concluding that significant declines of fertility in Asian villages within the near future are not possible.

A number of hypotheses emerge from the studies that have been made on fertility trends in underdeveloped countries:

(1) The possible role of the leaders of the community in movements toward restriction of fertility may be a critical factor in some large, economically undeveloped populations. In many parts of eastern and southern Asia, in contrast to situations in parts of Africa and western Asia, positive support of programs for the restriction of fertility would not necessarily involve any radical break with traditional social relations or cultural values.

(2) Community leadership is likely to have less importance and may be less critical in movements toward restriction of fertility in many parts of Latin America. Such movements here, in line with European experience, are likely to be largely spontaneous and individualistic.

(3) As the old sanctions for unlimited fertility break down under the impact of a new order, there may be

a renewed emphasis on the values and responsibility of family life, working toward the planning of family size.

(4) In some countries crisis situations may induce a rapid and widespread resort to drastic measures for reducing fertility. This has already happened in Japan and may be happening in China.

(5) Apart from crisis situations, the response of communities with positive but merely moderate interest in family limitation may be powerfully influenced by the acceptability of available means.

(6) The acceptability of various means now available for the control of fertility may vary widely in different cultures. This suggests the importance of experimentation with, and thorough investigation of, responses to various possible measures—including sterilization and rhythm as well as various contraceptive techniques.

III. RELIGIOUS TEACHING AND MORAL VALUES

1. Islam, Hinduism, and Buddhism

The contemporary situation in Islam, Hinduism, and Buddhism is such that these religions cannot be expected to give unified and clear-cut answers with respect to family limitation. Just as Christianity has produced many separate institutional religious groupings in its history, so too have Islam, Hinduism, and Buddhism. The problem is even more complicated in the case of the non-Western religions in that they have not had a conception of religious organization in the pattern of the Western world. There is no one individual or group which can speak authoritatively for any of these religions. They have not produced institutional forms which readily lend themselves to authoritative and representative statements.

The vast majority of the adherents of the non-Christian religions have not and do not face the problem of family planning or birth control with a vivid consciousness of its relationship to religious teaching and moral values. They are guided by the immediate situation which confronts them and by the custom morality of their society. It is usually only the intellectually alert religious person who views the problem in any of its ramifications beyond the particular individual's economic needs and social circumstances.

Modern Muslim thinkers have written much in an effort to show the wisdom and justice of the Prophet's teachings concerning the sexes and their relationships. They point out that in the teaching of Muhammad, marriage was instituted as a safeguard against sexual license and as a means of procreation. Paralleling the biblical injunction to be fruitful and multiply, Muhammad is recorded as saying "marry and generate," and also "marry a woman who holds her husband extremely dear, and who is richly fruitful." Thus at the very source of orthodox Muslim religious and social thought we have the basic conviction that a prime purpose of human life is the generation of new life. But there are some passages in the Koran that appear to support control of conception; and there are differences among important Muslim leaders today in this respect.

Hindu morality develops among the masses of the people on the level of caste custom and caste morality. For the Hindu caste member at all levels Karma, or the recognition that all actions have their consequences, is the binding authority which compels him to maintain the moral standards of his caste, both as a means of social relationship in his present life, and as an assurance of well-being in future lives. Most expressions of Hinduism are convinced that man is chained to a round of birth and rebirth.

Hinduism throughout the centuries of its existence has not been a morally demanding religion clearly challenging men with the requirements of an ethical God. It is not in the character of the Divine Itself that moral standards are primarily to be found, rather it is in the way of life decreed by the nature of human existence in a world where Karma, rebirth, and caste law (*dharma*) are authoritatively operative.

Buddhism from its earliest days constructed a system of moral living designed to aid the individual to limit or channel his desires and thereby reduce his suffering. The moral teachings of Buddhism as such are precepts which guide one in living a life of moderation, serenity, and adjustment. The average man lives the simple life wherein he seeks to follow the customs of his fathers. He appreciates the physical pleasures of life as much as any healthy man but ideally he does not make the error of allowing them to become the *summum bonum* of his existence.

When they have the opportunity, the people in the areas of each of these religions are responding to present-day problems of technology, population control, education, and like matters in a fashion similar to peoples in the areas of more technological advance. While we must not confuse the westernized cities of these areas with the village and rural populations which are the bulk of the peoples, yet even here the isolation from outside influences is rapidly disappearing. The partly westernized city dweller and the university student generation are important in these matters far beyond their numerical strength in that they are furnishing the bulk of the leadership for these areas. And despite great differences which must not be ignored, the masses of the people are not proving hostile to this leadership.

Custom morality, while receiving its content and form from the past, is not by that fact prevented from change and adaptation. Outside considerations or forces do cause a generation to question and to change the moral code it receives from its elders, particularly when such a change appears to guarantee a more pleasant material life. The change is not going to be achieved immediately if democratic processes are employed, but it must be remembered that custom morality by its very nature rests upon the will of the majority as well as upon the authority of the past.

There is a growing social conscience on the part of these religions and their contemporary leadership. Concern with poverty in its various manifestations forces consideration of population control to so great a degree that the religions themselves must not be ruled out as possible vehicles for its implementation.

In opposition to the foregoing factors these religions and their societies, being largely agrarian, have placed emphasis upon the duty to produce children, especially sons. This has received its authority from religious scriptures, from beliefs as to caste duty, and from the teachings of religious leadership. Their understanding of the nature of man and his place in the world has also furnished them authority for such emphasis. The religious belief and custom morality have been and are opposed to human interference with the processes of nature.

Islam has made and is making adjustments which would appear to indicate that the impulse to change existing conditions may also be considered an expression of Allah's will.

In the case of Hinduism the emphasis upon the religious duty of producing and raising children will not encourage population control except by continence. However, as we are aware, Indian political leadership at the present time is demonstrating a determination to make methods of family planning available to the population of India. Since orthodoxy is loosely defined in Hinduism, and rigorous conceptions of caste are breaking down, one would not expect Hinduism to be as adamant regarding planned parenthood as Islam.

Generally not concerned with teaching moral precepts among the laity, present-day Buddhism as such would not be expected to offer well-organized resistance to population control. The resistance would come from the custom morality of the areas in question.

If these religions are recognized as being in the process of adjustment, in which their fundamental presuppositions are not being given up but are being expressed in ways which are meaningful to their adherents in a rapidly changing world; and if it is perceived that these adherents are gradually, and in some cases eagerly, seeking to adjust to a world of new dimensions and meaning, then it is clear that attempts at the development of population control in their areas will meet problems which are different in degree, and not in kind, from the problems which population control meets in the Western world.

It is significant that the governments of India, Japan, and Egypt have set up Population Commissions charged with research and practical policies to meet their respective population problems.

2. *Fertility Control and Catholic Morality*

The emphasis in papal teaching has been placed on the finality of sex and marriage as such, on the ordering of various acts which lead up to procreation, and on respect for the human life which comes into being with conception. The Code of Canon Law formulates the ends of marriage thus: "The primary end of marriage is the procreation and education of offspring; the secondary end, mutual aid and the remedying of concupiscence."

At the same time the Catholic Church holds it proper for those who are fertile to regulate the use of marriage so that conception is less likely to result because they restrict relations to sterile periods. It is expected that each couple will be guided by their own convictions as to whether there are sufficient reasons of a social, economic, or other character, for delaying for a time or even permanently the procreation of children.

Evidently the person using artificial means of contraception, or otherwise taking positive steps to forestall conception, may intend to have more children and may actually have more children, than a Catholic in particular circumstances who is using the rhythm effectively for a good reason. The difference lies, so far as the Catholic Church is concerned, neither in the intent nor in the effect, but in the way the sexual act is performed. According to Catholic teaching, the finality of the act (and hence of the institution) is in one situation preserved; in the other it is subverted. Periodic abstinence or the rhythm method is legitimate where a sufficient reason exists for its regular practice. But other means are, according to Catholic teachings, immoral and seriously so.

On October 29, 1951, at Castel Gandolfo, the Pope delivered a discourse to the Italian Catholic Union of Midwives, from which we may quote as follows, using the words of the Pontifical Court Club's translation:

> Serious reasons, often put forward on medical, eugenic, economic, and social grounds, can exempt from that obligatory service (of having children) even for a considerable period of time, even for the duration of the marriage. It follows from this that the use of the infertile periods can be lawful from the moral point of view and, in the circumstances which have been mentioned, it is indeed lawful.

The Catholic Church approves studies on ways and means of using the rhythm more effectively. This implies research which will result in practical and simple methods of detecting with precision the exact time of ovulation, and sufficiently in advance that the risk of error, because of life of the sperm, is minimized.

Catholic morality will not approve the deliberate and direct destruction of fetal life. The Catholic Church also takes the position that the voluntary acceptance of sterilization, the act of sterilizing, and the promotion of sterilization as a means of contraception, are essentially wrong and that no legislation or act by public authority can make them right.

If physiologic control of fertility implies a direct interfering with biological processes in order to forestall meeting of sperm and egg, the Church holds it would not differ either in intent or in effect from other forms of artificial contraception. Conceivably there may be some types of physiologic means which would not imply such interference.

The totality of the Church's teaching includes a high esteem for virginity and celibacy and for a rational use of sex by the married. Thoughtless teen-age marriages, irresponsible childbearing, consensual marriages, legalized prostitution, easy divorce, are not approved as proper ways of behavior.

The Catholic Church has presented an organized doctrinal position on the responsibility of parents for the proper care of their children.

Non-Catholics should recognize that Catholic teachings in this field are grounded in deep theological principles. But within the limits established by papal decrees, which are accepted as authoritative within the Church, there are rather wide variations in emphasis and practice in the interpretation of these teachings in different situations. In particular, there appears to be some ambiguity as to whether or not married persons may have a personal or social obligation to refrain from procreation under some conditions. There is also deep concern among some Catholic thinkers about the problems created by rapid population increase in underdeveloped countries and the application of Christian principles to these problems.

3. Protestant Attitudes Toward the Control of Reproduction

Among Protestants there is not, nor can there be, an authorized belief regarding personal control of reproduction. Because Protestantism includes a multitude of denominations, there is no one official position set forth which is representative of Protestant faith or morals.

There have been very few statements by national or policy-making bodies of any of the denominations on the subject of the control of reproduction. The following are interpretations by men considered authorities in Protestant circles today and are representative of present trends in the thinking of the various non-fundamentalist Protestant denominations:

Dr. Leslie Weatherhead expresses himself in favor of birth control. Dr. Emil Brunner declares that nature indicates that God intended sexual intercourse as a means of expressing love as well as being the means of procreation. As for "birth control by self control," Dr. Brunner replies that asceticism is not a virtue and is absolutely contradicted by the admonitions of the Bible. This is not to condemn such a practice; if some prefer it to the use of contraceptives, that is their privilege. But they are not following any "better way," more pleasing in the sight of God.

Dr. Derrick Sherwin Bailey says, "Sexual intercourse is an act of the whole self which affects the whole self; it is a personal encounter between man and woman in which each does something to the other, for good or ill, which can never be obliterated. Sex is one of God's gifts to man and woman, and as such, is good in itself, and to be received with thanksgiving; there is no place for the unconsciously blasphemous attitude which regards the right use of sexual activity as something 'nasty' or 'impure.'" In general, Dr. Bailey's interpretation of the meaning of sex is representative of a trend among Protestant scholars.

A small booklet, recently developed for use among the young people of the Lutheran Church, and typical of at least twenty other pamphlets brought out by other denominations, says: "Keep in mind that children are a heritage from the Lord. Birth control is a privilege. It is not to be abused or used selfishly. Children are essential to the most successful marriage."

A recent joint statement by several Lutheran bodies in the United States includes the following: "An unrestrained production of children without realistic regard to God-given responsibilities involved in bringing children up 'in the discipline and instruction of the Lord' (Eph. 6:4) may be as sinful and as selfish an indulgence of the lusts of the flesh as is the complete avoidance of parenthood. God does not expect a couple to produce offspring at the maximum biological capacity. The power to reproduce is His blessing, not a penalty upon the sexual relationship of marriage."

It should not be overlooked that there are many Protestants who still regard sex itself as evil and the enjoyment of sexual experience as extreme worldliness. But the arguments advanced in some Protestant churches to oppose the limitation of reproduction are under heavy attack today by biblical theologians and social scientists. Protestant fundamentalism is yielding to change, and on the whole the Protestant churches in so far as they have formulated their thinking in this area, can be counted as quite strongly favoring the planning of family size.

4. Fertility, Religion, and Legislation in Europe

In most European countries, whether Catholic or non-Catholic, fertility is now so effectively controlled that less than one-half of the potential reproductive force of married couples actually finds expression in births. Countries clearly within this category (with notation of birth rates in 1956) are: Austria (16.4), Belgium (16.8), Denmark (17.2), Finland (20.8), France (18.3), West Germany (16.2), Greece (19.4), Italy (18.1), Netherlands (21.2), Norway (18.7), Spain (20.7), Sweden (14.8), Switzerland (17.5), United Kingdom (16.1). There can be no reasonable doubt that in most of these countries the control of fertility within marriage is effected chiefly by contraceptive practices. Family limitation through restriction to relatively sterile periods within the menstrual cycle may also be an important factor in some countries, but there is no definite information on this subject.

In contrast to such relative uniformity of behavior in the control of fertility in most European countries, their legal systems in this matter are radically different.

In the Scandinavian countries, including Finland, and in the United Kingdom there are no legal restrictions on contraceptive practices, and in some of these countries abortions are authorized on certain social as well as medical grounds. Information on contraception is provided in clinics under public auspices in a number of localities in northern Europe.

In many Catholic countries legislation intended to prohibit the dissemination of information on birth control and the sale of contraceptives stands in the statutes, in contrast to the actual practice of the people. Such legislation was established in France in 1920 and in Belgium in 1923 through the combined force of ecclesiastical interest in the defense of morality and of nationalistic interest in the maintenance of industrial and military manpower. But contraceptive supplies can be purchased without difficulty in these countries.

The disparity between legislation and behavior in this field raises grave doubts about the influence of legislation on ethical ideals and civic discipline. In many European countries restrictive legislation was associated with blatant nationalistic motives.

The closest agreement between ecclesiastic doctrine and popular practice prevails in Ireland, in conformity with a pattern of marriage and family relations that became prevalent under conditions of dire necessity in the mid-nineteenth century. Increase of family members is checked by severe postponement or avoidance of marriage. In 1951 only 41.6 per cent of the men aged 30-34 years and only 62.5 per cent of the women at these ages were married. Yet the illegitimacy rate is fairly low. There is, almost certainly, relatively little contraception or abortion. Thus it appears that about half of all young persons in Ireland pass 15 to 20 years after puberty without normal heterosexual relations, except perhaps for occasional lapses from the accepted pattern. This is a notable cultural achievement. Nevertheless, the question has been raised as to whether or not such deprivation is salutary.

5. Conclusions on Religious and Moral Influences

Outside of Europe and European settlements in other regions there is little organized religious or institutional opposition to the right of people to plan the size of their families. In most Asian countries political controversies over the use of contraceptives have been at a minimum. In contrast Europeans adopted birth control in the face of the opposition of most of the churches and even of secular legislation. In the more favorable climate of the Asian and Arab nations, population policies may develop on a sounder and more effective basis than has been the case in Europe or America. But long-established customs and habits need to be changed, and much inertia overcome.

There are great social changes now taking place in all the underdeveloped countries and these may offer local leaders unusual opportunities for the introduction of family planning.

In some Christian countries a deep split has been caused by the spontaneous movement toward family limitation in opposition to the traditional and revered principles of the Roman Catholic Church. The resulting tensions have led to strong pressures of a political nature. Most politicians avoid any issues which might arouse Catholic opposition. Individuals and groups espousing planned parenthood as a righteous cause stimulate counter forces. The conflict thus engendered acquires a political character that may compromise both the advancement of religious ideals and rational approaches to social problems.

This controversy has tended to obscure common ideals among different Christian communities and possibilities of cooperative action in advancing human welfare. Others must respect the loyalty of Catholic communicants to the teaching of their church, and recognize that in this teaching the only approved means of restricting births within marriage is continence, including periodic continence, "the rhythm method." They should appreciate the emphasis in Catholic training on the responsibility of parents for the nurture and education of children, the concern of the Roman Catholic Church about social conditions affecting human welfare, and the respect of its present leaders for freedom of scientific inquiry and the discussion of social issues.

At the same time there is reason to hope that in the future the Catholic Church may place greater emphasis on the affirmative teachings regarding the responsibilities of parenthood. It may also be hoped that in the future Catholic leaders will place less reliance on legislation and other coercive action by governments in this field.

Many Catholic leaders recognize the serious nature of the problems presented by current population trends in many countries. They also share with other religious leaders a deep concern for the positive values of family life. It may be hoped that a spirit of mutual respect and active cooperation in scientific inquiries may contribute to the advancement of constructive measures in meeting human needs in these fields.

Two: Indicated Lines of Action

IV. ASIA, AFRICA, AND THE ARAB STATES

A. Overcoming Cultural and Political Barriers

The major population problems of the contemporary world are in countries where the conditions of life are very different from those in Europe. The imperatives for survival in the densely settled river valleys and plains are similar in all the countries of Asia and the Middle East. They include local stability, life in close relation to the soil and the seasons, a careful husbanding of resources, and a familial unity in production and consumption. Closely related to the uniformities generated by their way of living are those associated with the biological processes of bearing and rearing children. The interrelations of family and other social and economic institutions are pervasive. Acceptance rather than rebellion is the proper attitude toward life and death.

The Westerners responsible for colonial policy did not wholly ignore problems of population pressure. There was considerable concern for the welfare of the people, and there was some realization of the problems of population increase. The Western people themselves were limiting their families, but this they regarded as personal. Contraception was not something that was talked about and advocated for others. Today new leaders in the East face the problems of a population growth which colonial influences failed to halt over the decades and the centuries.

Many of the responsible leaders of the new nations know the nature and dimensions of their population problems. They know that they dare not risk the continuation of rates of population growth of 2 and 3 and even 4 per cent per year. The problem is extremely difficult, and the subject is politically so hazardous that the cautious approach is essential for political leaders who wish to survive as such.

In the course of the discussions of the Committee, a group of experienced exchange teachers presently in Egypt, Lebanon, Jordan, Turkey, China, Japan, Indonesia, Mexico and Central America were asked to express their reactions to foreign efforts to promote family limitation. Their replies had the following in common:

. . . that national sensitivity to foreign efforts in this field is likely to reflect sensitivity to foreign activities generally, with reactions heightened because of the peculiarly personal nature of the issue;

. . . that national leaders tend to think in terms of resources-population ratios and thus, where population pressure is heavy, be ahead of general public opinion;

. . . that size of population is still considered one of the measures of national power.

Policies designed to increase or maintain fertility are flattering to the people who are urged to perpetuate themselves. But government policy which seeks the rapid reduction of fertility in the village populations is difficult both in adoption and in implementation. No government has yet dared the comprehensive policy that is openly, enthusiastically, and fully implemented. It is here that internal political forces become the greatest deterrent to population policy. And it is here that communist ideologies in the population field may be powerful and dangerous forces. But it should be noted that the Communist government of mainland China is developing a comprehensive population policy that involves not only contraception but abortion and sterilization as well.

The planning of family size should be part of a new concept of man's dignity, an integral aspect of moral progress in response to new opportunities and obligations created by the progress of science. But the danger increases that population growth might become *the* problem in underdeveloped areas as it did in Japan, and as it may be doing in China, with reduction of births torn from its relation to a finer family life and made a goal in its own right.

The awakening of peoples and the stimulations of governments present a challenge to imaginative idealism. The democratic belief in the supreme value of the individual life and in the right to equality of opportunity for all might well be integrated into a policy for a better family and individual life that was qualitative and developmental rather than crudely quantitative.

1. Some General Principles Relating to Cultural and Political Barriers

Certain general propositions may be advanced bearing on both government and private activities in the field of population.

(1) The reduction of population or the rate of population growth is not an end in itself but only a means of advancing the more general objective of human welfare.

(2) No family limitation program will be adopted in any country because of pressures from outside. Such attempts can only create antagonisms and the fuel for political propaganda.

(3) Because public health programs manifestly promote welfare and save lives, the public health services and the medical profession seem to provide the most promising vehicle for national and organized programs for controlling size of family.

(4) The actual practice of family limitation is a highly individual matter. It is adopted by the people themselves only for reasons of personal motivation, not for reasons of national advantage. Governments should not be too hastily criticized for failure to act, or to succeed, in programs of family limitation.

(5) The use of family limitation requires realization of need, it requires motivation, and it requires effective means. Programs in this sphere therefore often include education on purposes as well as the provision of means appropriate to the circumstances. Methods of family limitation must meet extremely difficult standards of practical feasibility within existing domestic arrangements; they must have aesthetic acceptability; they must be cheap, and must be to a substantial degree effective. We should be wary of what seem to be quick and simple solutions for a very complicated problem. Programs in the field of population will require patience, a persistent effort, tact, and rare good judgment.

2. *Possible Lines of Action*

Lines of action for encouraging parents to plan the size of their families will not be effective unless they take into account:

(1) the extreme sensitiveness of this highly personal subject;

(2) the spirit of nationalism which makes all countries unwilling to accept advice from foreigners.

The dangers of a too rapid growth of population as a whole and of the wrong distribution of births will be considered, not by the couples being asked to have smaller families, but by the leadership of the countries concerned, and on the basis of the evidence they themselves have gathered. On the other hand, public campaigns for family planning base their appeal on the health of mothers, better care and better opportunities for children, and on the improvement in family life. Fortunately the improvement of health and better child care are fields in which the goals are accepted without question.

Within this framework of psychological limitations, efforts to control family size are handicapped by the inadequacy of present methods for controlling conception. There is no magic pill, nor other means of simple physiological control, and there is no ground for believing that such solutions are just around the corner. Abortion, widely used in time of crisis, is certainly not an acceptable means; sterilization is at best a limited medical means. Main reliance must for the present be placed on methods of contraception which are only partly effective and not easily accepted, ranging from methods which are fairly effective but require materials out of reach of peasant populations, to incomplete intercourse which requires unusual self-control and to the rhythm method which is ineffective with untrained people.

Under these circumstances motivation becomes of paramount importance, together with the social conditions in which motivation can express itself in action. Perhaps it is fortunate that the underdeveloped countries are in a state of rapid revolutionary change. Many of the socio-economic adjustments now going on tend to foster smaller families. Among such are the enhanced status of women, opportunities for the employment of women outside the home, the spread of public education along rational and secular lines, and of course new standards of public health which tend to place a higher value on human life, lift standards of child care and promote child health. There are many ways in which an innovation that is generally wanted may be used as the carrier for values that are not immediately wanted but are ultimately necessary. Examples of this sort are found in public health and educational programs, in labor and social security legislation, in the organization of community development programs, in the form and content of industrial development, in channels of public communication, and in the tax structure.

The process of industrialization should of itself reduce the birth rate if we are to judge by Western experience. But Asia cannot afford the time this transition took in the West. We cannot be sure that industrialization will reduce births as much as it has in Western society, and no matter how rapidly industrialization may proceed, the enormous populations of the presently underdeveloped countries will be in the main tied to the land for a long time to come. The basic problem is concerned with peasant populations.

3. *Acceptable Foreign Contributions*

In any country the energy and resources directed to educating parents to plan the size of their families will depend heavily on the interest of political leaders and on the support they get from the people who form public opinion. Given an active interest on the part of all major articulate groups, it might well be possible to adopt a program that would reduce the birth rate with unprecedented speed. Without the backing of influential groups, political leaders will have to move cautiously lest they arouse strong opposition. One means of attaining wide public support is to promote an understanding of the demographic situation as it bears on the prospects of the individual family and of society as a whole for health, prosperity, and prestige. Since even these questions are heavily loaded with emotion it is doubtful that such an understanding can be based on the work of foreigners. For this reason it seems important that the nations equip their own scholars to study their problems with modern techniques. The stimulation of such work, and its interpretation for the informed public, should do much to secure the necessary political basis for the intelligent development of population policy.

At the level of leadership these problems arise as questions of population. Among the mass of the people they arise as questions of family health and well-being, of education and the improvement of living conditions. For these personal reasons the public will welcome programs for family planning even though the governmental interest derives from larger needs of the economy.

Basic research on population trends and their causes, if it is to be effective in stimulating leadership, needs to be done by trained indigenous personnel. In wide areas of the world, particularly those areas in which population problems are most acute, there is a major lack of social scientists, let alone social scientists trained in the field of population studies. Recently the United Nations has set up regional training centers in Chile and in India in which demographers from neighboring countries can be trained by competent teachers at a lower expense than that necessary in Western universities. The results will not be felt at once, but in the long run solutions are most likely to be found by local personnel, trained at the highest academic level.

In addition to the training of personnel, and partly as a means of training, there needs to be a wide range of experiments and field trials designed to find the most efficient means of influencing behavior in a wide variety of situations. Knowledge of the social and psychological factors affecting fertility and of the attitudes, motivations and cultural patterns in different areas is an essential preliminary to sound programs of action. There have been a number of such studies carried out in the United States, and recently studies of this sort have been made in the Caribbean, in Japan, and in India. The studies in India promise much information useful to the operation of a growing program of family planning clinics under the Ministry of Health. The Japanese studies have furnished a dramatic example of methods which effect a subsitution of contraception for abortion among some of the lowest income groups in Japan. The Egyptian government is now carrying on a program of training personnel for the conduct of studies among the peasant population of the Nile.

In addition to the value of the information obtained,

such studies have the effect of stimulating interest in problems of population, and have value in the training of personnel.

4. Needed Medical Research

There are two types of medical problems relating to population which are needed to supply information for general use in all areas. For these the United States with its wealth and great number of technical schools has a particular responsibility, which unfortunately it is far from meeting. The first or at least the most immediate problem relates to the existing means of family limitation under various conditions; their acceptability, their safety, and their effectiveness; and in the case of contraceptives, to specifications, standards, manufacturing methods, and costs of the different types of materials now being used. Most of the studies of the effectiveness of various types of contraceptives are of a clinical sort, many of them statistically unreliable, some of them biased, and only recently has there been any central source of information on their meaning. The method of periodic continence, the so-called rhythm method, has never been sufficiently studied. More knowledge of how to determine the precise time of ovulation would be a great help to those who wish to use this method.

Of far greater long-run importance is the study of the physiology of reproduction. This is an area in which scientific knowledge is currently inadequate. Added knowledge would help improve maternal health throughout the world, would help reduce premature births and spontaneous abortions, and should make available means of controlling family size which would be more acceptable than any now available, and more effective, and cheap enough for universal use. The search for a physiological means of fertility control has been likened to the search for a means of controlling cancer. The two problems are not unlike, in that both are concerned with the processes of cell growth, and both concern specific cells which must be interfered with without disturbing the other cells of the body. There are a number of leads, but no early prospect of solution.

The total amount of money being spent on research on reproduction is very small compared to the need, a fraction of that spent on any one of the major diseases.

B. Methods and Means of Influencing Leadership

Decisions as to size of family are made by couples for highly personal reasons. The most pervasive influence is undoubtedly the culture in which they live; the traditions which have been handed down, the attitudes of their friends and neighbors. These things are changed by contacts with the outside world and by their local leadership. In isolated and largely illiterate communities, such as those where a large proportion of the world's people are found today, attempts at outside interference are looked on with suspicion and may harden rather than change existing attitudes. Mass education thrives only on indigenous soil, and must be undertaken by local leadership. The intellectual respectability of ideas, as endorsed by leaders in terms of patriotism and piety, may be of greater importance in determining acceptability in areas of low literacy and education than in a society where more of the people are able to deal with intellectual concepts of their own.

For these reasons, and because local cultures present complicated patterns, different not only from country to country but from area to area, those interested in the introduction of new ideas will be well advised to work with the leadership rather than directly with the masses.

1. The Reservoir of Leadership

The question naturally arises—who are the leaders? In countries with a high proportion of literacy the influential leadership may not be easy to identify, for the general public often does not know who the real leaders are. A number of studies have been made recently to find means of locating the real intellectual leaders in the United States. But in the less developed countries it is probably safe to start with the assumption that the educated classes, the "intellectual elite," include practically all the leaders, and that ideas circulating in the intellectual group in general will almost surely touch the leaders of tomorrow. There has been, as yet, no tendency for Asian leaders to rise up from complete obscurity.

2. The Requirements of Leadership

In matters of population Asian leaders are, as we know, frequently ahead of popular opinion. But they may be timorous about taking action for which there will be no following. They need an intellectual constituency for their ideas. The leaders need the comfort and encouragement of an informed group of intellectuals to confirm them in their faith. The nationalistic views of their constituents require that new ideas be given an indigenous background, fully thought out and appropriate to local conditions, and in the framework of accepted national policy.

The local auspices for any movement of ideas must be real, not counterfeit. It is essential that the ideas be arrived at by conviction, not by rote. It would therefore seem important that thinking on population problems should develop as a natural sequence to considerations which are already acceptable.

3. Effective Approaches to the Population Problem

The concept of rational planning in general is one of the easiest to present in Asia. Conservation and increase of productivity are equally acceptable. With these as a basis there need be no a priori assumption that the control of births is a good thing. The logic of planning will lead inevitably to exactly that conclusion. In planning an increase in the food supply, it will soon be evident that a large increase in gross production might be more than offset by a too rapid growth of population. Progress in industrialization is affected by the proportion of the labor force to the total population, the proportion of workers being higher at lower rates of fertility. Thus the idea of the need for the control of fertility follows as a natural deduction from the aspirations for improvement now so general throughout the African and Asiatic worlds. Agencies appropriate to this approach would include those in the fields of economic planning, agricultural economics, conservation, statistics, general sociology, child and family welfare, educational planning, and economic geography, to mention the most appropriate.

Public health is also a natural framework on which

to build an awareness of the advantages of smaller families. There is no form of human society in which mothers do not care about the welfare of their children. Higher ideals of child care, of sanitation and nutrition are among the first requirements of a campaign of public health. As these ideals are generally accepted, the large family becomes increasingly a recognizable handicap, while at the same time more of the children survive and large families are no longer necessary for the continuation of the family line.

The public health approach, unlike the others, is not only appropriate to the leadership, but brings the question of family size directly to the masses. Illiteracy does not prevent a mother from recognizing that if she gives her children proper care more of them will survive, and that too many children limit her ability to care for any of them properly. This approach is particularly appropriate to doctors, nurses, and midwives. In most of Asia, the Arab countries, Africa, and South America, physicians do not reach the mass of the people. But almost everywhere midwives are important because of their close contact with the people; and public health nurses, where they are found, may also have great influence.

4. Communist and Other Misconceptions

As late as 1954 "birth control" was anathema to Communist governments. But by 1955 and 1956 the leaders of Communist China found that their plans for industrialization and the increase of the food supply could not be successful unless a limit were put on the growth of population. An active campaign to reduce the number of births is now being carried on by the Chinese government. The conversion of the Communist leadership to the necessity of limiting family size came about through the process of deduction from planning for other things, but has been wisely publicized as a health and welfare measure. The Chinese government has thus placed itself on the side of those who seek to improve the quality of family life.

In addition to bringing the need of family limitation to leaders through such processes as we have indicated, it is desirable to correct a number of erroneous ideas which are very generally held. Many Europeans and a number of American leaders undoubtedly still believe that gross population is an index of national power, and this false idea is probably widely held in other countries. The idea is false because if population is out of balance with resources and productivity, the extra population can be a serious handicap. And in so far as population growth exceeds the growth of production, growth is an index of national weakness, not of power.

Nor is a high proportion of large families a sign of biological vigor, as so often asserted by Hitler and others. There is no evidence of differences in capacity to breed between different races of peoples. Differences in average size of family between large groups are determined by social and psychological influences. After mortality has been reduced, a high birth rate is too often the concomitant of ignorance and low levels of living, rather than a sign of vitality or progress.

5. *Processes of Education*

In the European countries and in Japan family limitation came about through private word of mouth rather than through official and political propaganda. To a great extent this will probably be the case in the villages under the direction of local leadership. Even mass education reaches mainly the more literate and educated groups. Mass education may take the form of feature articles by science writers submitted for publication in newspapers and periodicals of wide circulation. Such materials are widely accepted by Asian journals, and there is an urgent need that they should be tailored to the cultural imperatives of each country and region. More popular educational materials, such as comic books, wall posters, films, radio, and TV, may often be effective under local sponsorship.

At a later stage it should be possible to get better materials on population translated and published in cheap editions. But even here it is desirable to present the problems, and not to propagandize the solutions. Material for the masses should be couched in local terms. While individual decisions about size of family are made on the basis of immediate personal interest and under local social pressures, this is not to say that patriotic and religious factors have no influence on individual couples. Often such factors determine the acceptability of a new idea such as the idea of limiting the number of one's children.

As in the case of the lonely leader, the individual citizen needs assurance that a personally attractive course is not inconsistent with locally accepted canons.

6. *Some General Considerations*

It is not easy to capture the attention of people for a subject in which they are not already interested, and to break through their resistance to persuasion. Different methods apply among different peoples, but there are some general rules which apply in most situations. Communications agreeing with the individual's predispositions, and which are not likely to be contradicted, are most effective when presented in a one-sided manner. But communications to a group whose predispositions are such that they are likely either to hear or to think of objections are often more effective if the expectable objections are answered in the initial communication. Communications which raise anxiety may persuade less than those which do not, because anxiety-engendering information is apt to be forgotten.

There is another general rule about communication which bears particularly on communication from foreign sources. People are apt to identify a message with the source of the message. If the source produces what seems to them an inappropriate communication, either the attitude to the source must change, or the communication will be forgotten. When the source is likely to be looked on with suspicion, it is particularly important that the message not go beyond terms which are already acceptable and understandable. Population information which elicits local images will have a more significant and lasting impact than will the same information couched in terms which elicit foreign images.

It is not easy to transfer a new idea from one group to another, and even harder when it is in effect a new way of life. In spite of many troubles, the atmosphere of Asia at present is favorable to creative thinking. The growth of literacy and education leads to a quicker dethronement from power of the old generation. New ideas have a readier chance of acceptance. The general climate seems favorable to an understanding of the problems of population.

V. THE UNITED STATES, CANADA, AND A COMPARISON WITH THE SOVIET UNION AND OTHER INDUSTRIALIZED COUNTRIES

The combined area of the continental United States today and its northern neighbor, Canada, comprises about one-seventh of the land area of the earth. The Soviet Union covers about one-sixth of the earth's land area, though in a colder region and with less rainfall. The combined populations of Canada and the United States were about 188 million in 1956 and that of the Soviet Union about 200 million.

Each of these areas is highly industrialized. Each has a higher proportion of cultivable land and natural resources to people than any other part of the world excepting only Australia. Europe with less than half the land of either of these areas has somewhat more people and is highly industrialized, but lacks the resources of either Russia or the United States and Canada. All these areas are in the process of rapid industrial expansion. The people of North America and the Soviet Union, though numbering together less than one-sixth of the world's population, already produce and consume much more than one-half of the world's goods other than food. Each is already drawing to some extent on the raw materials of the rest of the world. Each is trying to raise higher still the level of living of their people.

In an immediate sense these areas do not have a population problem. But for the longer term the way they handle their population problems may be important not only to their own people, but also to the well-being and even to the peace of the world as a whole.

In the case of the Soviet Union our present information is insufficient for a careful analysis. But a discussion of the problem as it appears in the United States may throw light on some of the problems of population growth in the Soviet Union as well as in Canada, and to a less degree on the problems of industrialized Europe.

1. Economic Aspects of Population Growth in the United States

Through much of American history public opinion seems to have favored the maximum expansion of the population to fulfil the "Manifest Destiny" of the nation to occupy an almost empty continent. This spirit encouraged new enterprise and new methods of production. Growth made possible a greater use of mass production and provided the psychological base for optimism about the future. With a small population and unlimited resources, growth was a factor contributing to the increase of per capita production in the United States.

Perhaps there are still advantages to be gained by further increases in the number of people in the United States. Continued growth will make possible larger scale production, and encourage business to make new investments in productive enterprises. But this does not mean that individual consumers would benefit by being more numerous. It is doubtful that further growth would be a factor making for increase in the income of individuals. We are at the point in our population-resources ratio where pressure of larger numbers upon scarce natural resources lays a restraining hand on increases in per capita production, which can be offset only for a limited time by technical advances and the use of new capital.

Capital and resources are absorbed in taking care of the needs of a growing population, as for instance in housing and schools, and additional capital is required to build up the larger production facilities needed to provide goods for more people. When, as at present, the population of the United States is growing at the rate of 1.8 per cent a year, savings representing some 6 per cent or more of the national income would have to be used each year to offset these requirements of growth, were it not for technological advances.

The proportion of men and women at labor force ages is lower (55 per cent of the whole) in a population which is growing at the rate of 1.5 per cent a year, as in the United States, than in a non-growing stable population (70 per cent). Because of this effect on age structure, growth may constitute a handicap to the economy.

Population growth entails a high proportion of children to the rest of the population. In the United States parents generally make an effort to provide the best possible education, medical care, and nutrition for each child. The money spent on their children may come to a high proportion of the family income. If there are many children compared to the number of adults, as is the case in a rapidly growing population, the community is burdened and real sacrifices are required of the family. The unexpected increase in births since 1940 has created a shortage of school buildings and of teachers which will not be remedied for a long while to come and has increased local taxes many fold.

Finally, population growth makes the cost of raw materials higher. The United States is depleting its natural resources with unprecedented speed, and there is reason to fear serious shortages of certain materials in the near future, and these shortages will be much accentuated by the demands of a larger population. But to a considerable extent this danger is offset by the possibilities of substitution, aluminum for copper, taconite ore for the iron ores of Lake Superior, concrete and stone for wood, plastics from air and water. Higher costs will bring out new materials and pay for extraction from lower grade sources. At present the cost of raw materials is about 5 per cent of the cost of finished products in the United States. A doubling of this cost would certainly bring out an enormous amount of additional or substitute materials. The cost of living would be increased, though not unduly. But if the United States population reaches 250 million to 350 million as seems likely in the next fifty or one hundred years, shortage of raw materials might become a serious threat to the level of living.

Energy sources have the same elastic quality. Slight increases in cost can bring about the substitution of oil from shale for oil from wells, of chemicals from coal instead of from oil, thus saving oil. New technological advances which have already brought near the use of atomic power, may make possible the direct utilization of energy from the sun and other sources now unused.

The food production of the United States has been affected by technological advances perhaps even more than has industrial production. Since 1900 food production has increased by 50 per cent while the agricultural labor force has decreased by two-fifths and there has been an actual decrease in harvested acreage. The most striking examples have been in wheat, corn, and cotton. Harvested acreage of wheat is down since 1900 from 58 million acres to 50 million, while wheat production is up 19 per cent. Harvested acreage of corn is down from 100 million acres to 79 million acres with production way up, while cotton acreage is down from 42 million acres to 16 million acres with no decline in production. The proportion of people living on farms has declined from about 90 per cent of the population in 1800, to 35 per cent in 1910 and to about 13 per cent in 1955, and there is a surplus of foodstuffs. But the efficiency of agriculture cannot increase at this rate indefinitely. With continued growth of population in the United States and a diminishing proportion of land to people, there will come a point when the trend will change and food costs will go up.

There is one rational reason which can be advanced for a further growth which would lower individual consumption but increase gross production. It can be argued that larger numbers and a larger plant would put the United States in a better position to survive in a war. But even this position may not be wholly tenable, for modern war seems to require technical proficiency rather than numbers.

The United States still has a relatively low ratio of population to land area and natural resources. It has a tremendous and growing industrial plant. It is conditioned to rapid technological change. For some time to come these factors will modify or offset the handicaps imposed by the growth of population. It is understandable that economists do not foresee any lowering of present levels of living during the next twenty-five years, even if growth should continue at the present high rate. The United States appears able to support a population of from 250 million to 300 million toward which, barring unexpected catastrophe, it is headed in the next twenty-five to fifty years. With that larger base the future may look more threatening. Forecasts beyond twenty-five to thirty years have little meaning. But the optimism engendered by the recent baby boom is justified, if you will, in terms of business expansion; it is not justified in terms of benefits to the individual consumer.

2. *Effect of Further Population Growth on the Quality of the American People*

Education is open to all the people of the United States, and standards of education are high compared to those in other countries. Standards of home and medical care are also high, as are standards of nutrition. But whatever levels people actually enjoy, it is natural for them to aspire to a higher level, and the American people are no exception. They want to give their children even better care. They want more and better schools and more and better teachers, and they want all children to enjoy whatever type of education their particular abilities entitle them to. These things all contribute to improving the quality of the people. But they cost money, and their cost is in proportion to the ratio of children to adults in the population. A high proportion of larger families and a too rapid rate of population growth often means that neither the individual parents nor the community can meet the cost of education and health services, and the quality of the people begins to suffer.

American institutions, ranging from government at the federal, state, and local level, through the churches and through the innumerable private welfare agencies, have been slow to recognize the changes inevitably flowing from the recent great reduction in child mortality. Little or nothing has been done to discourage large families among the least educated and least responsible parents. At the same time the mass of responsible people have gradually over the last hundred years come to think of two or three children as the ideal number. This has had some unfortunate results. Many less thoughtful parents, careless about the upbringing and education of their children, have continued to have large families without social penalty and apparently with the approval of society. A disproportionate number of children tends, in each generation, to be born to a group of parents who are socially handicapped either through ill health, poverty, incompetence, low mental ability, or emotional disturbance. The children in these disadvantaged families contribute more than their proportion of juvenile delinquency, and have a retarding effect on education. They tend to lower in each generation the quality of the people.

3. Some Advantages of Space and Wealth

Many deep human needs are related to available space. Different people and different societies value space in different terms. Many early Americans felt crowded if there were neighbors within a couple of miles of their farm. City dwellers want only "a little more" space for lawns, playgrounds, and parks, a little less crowd on the sidewalks and streets. Most people want more parks, more beaches, larger and more numerous recreation areas. This need is most acutely felt in the great urban and suburban areas of the United States, which are constantly more crowded with people. But even the great national parks of the United States as well as the state and local parks, are now crowded beyond their capacity, and more are demanded. Loss of space means a loss in the quality of living which Americans have always previously enjoyed.

There are other and less tangible aspects to the diminishing ratio of space to population in the United States. It can be argued that some of the most valuable qualities in American life have arisen under the influence of the uncrowded openness of the country. Do our open spaces contribute to the sense of individuality, of independence, of originality and adjustment to change? Can these be maintained under the crowded conditions which would prevail if the country were to have three or four hundred million inhabitants? There is some doubt, too, about the effect of further crowding on the functioning of democratic forms of government in so large a country. Space has helped to give the American people a sense of confidence in the future, a feeling of optimism, of security for their children. No one can forecast how they will change as the space around them becomes more limited.

Wealth like space has effects which may be good or ill, depending on how wealth is distributed and used. During the whole period of its growth the United States has had the advantage of great quantities of readily available natural resources, sufficient until very recently to supply the majority of its own needs, even with the immense resource requirements of the system of mass production. The favorable balance of its population to its resources has been one of the major factors making possible an unparalleled per capita production of goods.

This great flow of goods has encouraged a mass distribution beyond any attained in the past. Accompanying this distribution has been a constantly greater equalization of levels of living, and this not at a level of scarcity, but at a level of comfort and decency. Finally this has meant in actual practice that more and more people are enjoying and taking part in the cultural life of the country to an extent never known before except among small and specially favored groups.

With the technological changes already in sight and those which may be expected in the future there is every reason to hope that these trends toward an equalization of goods at a higher level of comfort and security and a continuing increase in cultural opportunities may continue into the future. It would be a demonstration on a large scale of the possibilities for reaching a level of quality in human living which has hitherto seemed an unattainable goal.

At present no area other than that of the United States with its low ratio of population to resources is in a position to achieve this goal in such measure. If it should be achieved in the United States, it might provide a great stimulus toward improving the relation between numbers and resources in other areas, with a consequent improvement in the quality of human life. War or some other calamity may prevent such a hoped-for fulfilment. So may a long continued growth in numbers. It would be a tragedy for mankind if this unique opportunity should be lost as a result of uncontrolled growth of population.

4. Has the United States a Population Policy?

In the early days of the United States, when there were few people in the country and a vast expanse of unoccupied land, the birth rate was very high. Most women were married and married women averaged six and sometimes as high as eight children apiece. Families of fifteen to twenty were not unknown. Though the death rate was high the population was doubling every twenty-five years.

Gradually, as the country began to fill up, as industry grew and people moved to the cities, as levels of living and education were raised, people began having fewer children. During the depression of the 1930's the women of the United States were having barely enough children to replace their own number in the next generation. The downward trend was reversed early in the 1940's by an increase in births in the white collar groups and for more than ten years births have remained substantially above prewar levels, though still much below the level of births before World War I. It remains to be seen whether this reversal is permanent.

The higher birth rate has continued through the 1950's, though we cannot as yet tell the size of the completed families of women married so recently. Economic, sociological, and psychological factors were apparently responsible for the rise. The number of marriages was increased by a reduction in age at marriage, and the proportion of first and second children born each year increased accordingly. The proportion of four-child families increased slightly, but the proportion of families of five, six, or more children has continued to decline. Average size of completed family in 1955 was 2.8 per married woman, up by almost one-third since the great depression of the thirties. It is possible, perhaps even probable, that the postwar increase in births is a temporary upsurge in the long decline since colonial days. The baby boom has already ceased in Europe, and may cease in the United States. But this would only mean that the American population was growing more slowly, not that it had ceased its growth.

The reduction in the birth rate which took place in the past hundred years in the United States was the result of decisions by individual parents that they would limit the size of their families. The method used has been some form of contraception, including the rhythm method. The change has not been encouraged by any government or state, nor by the churches, nor by any of the traditional institutions of the country. There has been no policy for the reduction of births. The smaller family came as the natural reaction of people to changed conditions of life. It took a long time for them to change their traditional attitudes, almost a hundred years. And the change is not entirely complete, for there are still isolated areas and groups with the birth rates of a hundred years ago.

Many factors are responsible for the declining birth rates in the period prior to World War II. Among them are higher standards of child care, concern for the health of the mother, higher standards of living, changed values associated with urbanization and industrialization, and possibly a reaction to the further reduction in deaths of children. There were no population policies as such at the governmental level, nor were any established institutions concerned with population, though isolated birth control groups were making a valiant effort to spread the use of contraception. But the government carried out many policies which undoubtedly affected population trends even though that was not their intent.

The early freedom of immigration to the United States was an expression of the feeling that the United States should be a haven for all those seeking a better life. Later an expanding industry welcomed immigrants as a source of much needed labor. Finally the fear that more immigrants could not be assimilated aroused a public reaction, and immigration was put on a quota system where it has since remained. Through all the early periods, immigration affected population trends in many ways, particularly by the high birth rate of the first generation of immigrants.

Another government policy which affected population, though not designed for that purpose, was the system of government land grants. Western lands were thrown open to homesteaders without cost, and the movement of population westward was greatly accelerated as a result. The conditions of life on the frontier made for larger families than the same parents would have had in the more crowded East, and the high birth rate further expanded the western settlement.

Other government policies have also affected the distribution of population. The construction of the Erie Canal gave great impetus to the westward movement of the American people, and later government encouragement of railroad expansion hastened by many years the settlement of western areas in which birth rates remained high for a long period. In the same way the railroad rate system fixed by the government, and the construction of roads and waterways, were factors which affected the distribution of industry and hence of population and trends in growth.

The psychological climate of the environment at any particular time is important in determining the number of children people will have. Many things must enter into this climate; they need to be studied for their effect on population growth. At present we can only list those factors which may be suspected of exerting an influence, without trying even to indicate whether the effect of any particular influence is to encourage or to discourage births. Such a list might include:

A public school system which puts the minimum of additional burden on parents carrying their children through grade and high school, but is expensive at the level of college and particularly expensive at the graduate level—and the accompanying system of scholarships.

Federal income tax exemptions for dependent children.

Social security, unemployment, sickness, disability insurance and old age pensions, and aid to dependent children.

City planning, urban renewal, and slum clearance projects, and the size of the rental units subject to subsidy.

Regulations concerning marriage and divorce, a variety of social agencies, family and marriage clinics.

Exemption of married men with children from the draft, together with liberal provisions for care of army dependents.

This list is neither exhaustive nor does it necessarily include the factors which are most influential. The list is important only as it offers examples of the kinds of things that must be taken into account if government policies are to be developed in a way to have a favorable effect on population trends.

5. *Conclusions re the United States*

Given a balance of population and resources such as there is in the United States today, sound population policy requires not the enunciation of a "population policy" but rather the systematic evaluation of all sorts of public measures and programs for their effect on marriage, birth rates, and death rates. In the United States the idea of family limitation is widely accepted and contraceptive methods are readily available. The great majority of married couples in the United States may be expected, with some further education in this matter, to adjust the size of their families to their own best interests, including the health of both mother and children. The adjustment should be in the best interests of society as well if the laws, institutions, and social customs which affect population are soundly conceived from the point of view of population policy.

An evaluation of government policies is necessary not only for their effect on the numbers, but also for their effect on the quality of the American people. Government policies should be of a sort to equalize births between people at different socio-economic levels. They should discourage births among the socially handicapped who cannot give their children adequate opportunities. They should encourage large families among the specially gifted. Ultimately government policies may seek to encourage genetic improvement from one generation to another. But much research is needed in this field. At present the only indicated genetic policy would be the establishment of heredity counselling services for the voluntary use of parents seeking advice. To make such services effective, there is need for a change in the point of view of the public as to the right of carriers of genetic defects to have children when it is known that their children, or some substantial proportion of them, will have serious genetic defects.

The United States and Canada occupy a unique position, shared only by the Soviet Union, Australia and New Zealand, in that their present balance of population to natural resources is still favorable to a continuing increase in the well-being of their people.

But if present rates of growth should continue for as long as another two generations, both the United States and the Soviet Union will be reduced to a position in which the balance of population to resources may seriously handicap the effort to improve the level of living. They would then lose what is perhaps their major advantage over the other large but more heavily populated areas of the world.

There is little evidence that either the United States or the Soviet Union recognizes the direction in which it is moving. The United States is a backward country with respect to population policy. American political leaders are unaware of the problems, or are afraid to face them. It is not discussed freely and naturally as in many other countries. It is only by the unique nature of its early growth, and because of the present levels of education and economic aspiration of its people, and not by any intelligent development of policy, that the United States has slowly reduced its birth rate to a closer balance with the rate of deaths.

The rest of the world cannot but watch the further population growth of the United States and of the Soviet Union with interest and some anxiety. Not because a doubling of their numbers (toward which they are now heading) would strongly tend to lower their level of living. That is something for the American and Russian people to worry about. But the continued growth of population in these highly industrialized areas, as indeed in Europe, will make for increasing demands on the world's resources, and this is properly a matter of world concern. In the not distant future these problems which involve resources as well as people may become a major issue for discussion in the United Nations.

In the less highly industrialized areas of the world in which today live more than a majority of the world's people, a continued growth of population means immediate hardship and privation for the couples with large families who are the cause of the growth. All those who care about human well-being cannot but be deeply concerned. This brief statement has been written in the hope that it may provide a better understanding of the problems involved and of the means of solving them.

INDEX